Business English Writing

....

Grammar, exercises and vocabulary
for business communication.
Increase the skills to write and speak at work.

Guide for managers and business leaders.

•

MASTERCLASS INTERNATIONAL SCHOOL

....
Copyright © 2020 Masterclass International School
All rights reserved.

Introduction 9

Organization of The Text 11

Some Observations About Language 13

British English, American English and Other Varieties of English 17

Chapter 1 EMPLOYEES TEAM BUILDING 20

Chapter 2 EMPLOYEES STAFF MOTIVATION 42

Chapter 3 COMPANIES START-UPS 60

Chapter 4 ACTIVITIES MARKETING 94

Chapter 5 INTERCULTURAL COMMUNICATION NEGOTIATION 108

Chapter 6 PEOPLE MONEY 131

Chapter 7 PEOPLE STRATEGIES 153

Chapter 8 PEOPLE SUCCESS 179

Chapter 9 PEOPLE JOBS 194

Chapter 10 COMPANIES TRENDS 213

Chapter 11 ACTIVITIES DISCUSSING ISSUES 227

Chapter 12 ACTIVITIES DESCRIBING PEOPLE AND THINGS 236

Appendix 1 253

Appendix 2 258

Masterclass International School

Introduction

Before working on this new Business English Writing text, I asked myself several questions, two or three of which surfaced more than others in my mind, causing doubts and perplexities. The first question concerned what exactly I should offer the reader in the book, while the second asked how I could organize the material to create a dynamic and above all useful text.

My passion for the subject, supported by the need to provide new perspectives for study and linguistic reflection to the student, led me to justify the preparation of Business English Writing, which fits into the panorama of English teaching for purposes special and, in particular, business English.

In the current working landscape, although characterized by a difficult economic situation, English continues to maintain its role as an international language, used for international trade and for many other activities related to the business world.

Therefore, today's students will certainly continue to have to do with business English and especially those who will have the "luck" to work in a company or in a reality where it is necessary to use the language of specialty with a certain ease.

Business English Writing can be more generally a valid reference tool also for those who want to improve their skills in the micro-language of business, driven by the professional opportunities that the knowledge of English offers, thus keeping their English updated where it already represents a precious daily work tool.

Therefore, Business English Writing is not configured as a text for a limited audience. My work has focused on the search for material suitable above all for people whose knowledge of the business-economic world is still limited, in the process of being trained and who, precisely for this reason, do not necessarily have to sectorise their linguistic knowledge at this stage (pre-experienced learners). But even for those who already work professionally (managers, accountants, consultants and other specialists), I can believe that they will find a stimulating material, useful for deepening the business language outside of those technicalities that (probably) they already know because they are an integral part of the their job (job-experienced learners).

The activities and exercises present in the various units seek to stimulate the student not so much to theoretical language learning, but to active communication in English and to reflection on the issues of greatest interest for modern businesses.

Organization of The Text

Business English Writing is divided into twelve units inspired by the company and the human resources that work in it, taking into consideration the globalized reality in which we live today. Each unit focuses on a topic (new businesses, personnel management, marketing, negotiation and so on), at the basis of which there is a newspaper, magazine or specialized website article.

This is followed by a range of activities related to the development of the four language skills, although greater attention has been paid to oral skills (especially the development of the speaking skill).

Therefore, the activities of the various units revolve around the initial article, often accompanied by a glossary of different types (more or less complete according to the purposes required by the related activities).

The new words are inserted in the exercises and in the example sentences (in the part called grammar revision) to encourage the student to acquire a more natural acquisition of the new lexicon.

Most of the units focus on a grammatical topic providing a brief reference to theory, followed by a series of related exercises, which are still useful for linguistic reasoning and consolidation of the proposed structures.

The text also presents a series of supplementary activities, mostly related to listening skills. Practical links to the articles are provided in many of the proposed units and in this the student's personal initiative can also contribute significantly to improving their oral comprehension skills.

Some Observations About Language

When studying a language, especially at an advanced level, it is necessary to consider words from a new perspective, a broader viewpoint with regard to the following aspects: basic meaning, polysemy, synonymy, collocation, connotation and register as well as the geographical variety of the language, e.g. British English, American English, etc.

Every word has a basic meaning, so if we were to analyse a sentence such as Along with our customers, the main asset of the company is that we are a highly motivated, committed and capable force and we didn't understand the meaning of a word, of course we could look it up in a dictionary where we could find the explanation. Let us suppose that the unknown word is asset; the dictionary would give the following definition: anything valuable or useful (English), or another word with a similar meaning: possession (English).

This is the basic meaning of the word, but more often than not words can have other meanings, and this is what we call polysemy. A polysemous word has multiple meanings, just like the word asset which also means stock (2), advantage (3), resource (4). The meaning (1) is often found in the plural form assets, that is any property owned by a person or firm (English). This is just an example of how many different meanings words can have and this is true for other lexical items in the sentence we have taken into consideration. Of course, the context is often helpful in understanding the word when spoken or in a piece of writing.

Another characteristic of words is synonymy. Synonyms are words with a very similar but slightly differing meaning. For example, the word customer has some synonyms in client, patron, consumer, shopper, buyer, user. Sometimes these words are interchangeable, so you can decide to use one or another, but this is not always true. While customer and client are now very similar – someone who buys products or services - the word patron is mostly used for habitual customers of bars and restaurants. But in spite of the fact that the word customer can always replace the word patron, the opposite is not true.

Another typical aspect of words is that they are often accompanied by a fixed set of words, so they are used with each other more frequently. Collocations are common word combinations. For example the adjective motivated is often accompanied by extremely, highly, strongly, very, well. This is the reason why new vocabulary should not be learned as an isolated part of the language, but together with the word with which it is associated.

Connotation has to do with the associations that are linked to a certain word, the emotional aspect that word evokes, which opposes the literal meaning of the word, called denotation or the dictionary definition. For example, the word rose refers to a specific type of flower, but symbolically it can recall love and passion. Another example may be given by adjectives. If you wish to describe someone as refusing to comply or agree, which of the following adjectives would you use? stubborn, unyielding, headstrong, obstinate, dogged, resolute, adamant, pertinacious, pig-headed, persistent, unwavering, resolute, firm. And which of the above adjectives would you use to define someone who has determination or strength? Be careful! Words may have a similar denotation but a different connotation.

Another important language aspect is register. It is the style related the purpose, audience and social context where communication takes place. It has to do with the degree of formality in use, so a formal register would require something like Mr. Smith, would you like a cup of tea?, whereas in friendly, informal context we could just say Paul, want some tea? The context regulates register which will basically be formal or informal.

As for the geographical variety of the language, we should remember that what is commonly said in Britain may differ from what is said in America, in Canada or in Australia as well as in other English speaking countries. American English tends to be the most dominant variety in the world nowadays and some American words are also used or understood by speakers of other varieties of the language, but sometimes this does not happen. Barrister, biscuit and flyover are British English; the same words in American English are attorney, cookie and overpass. Apart from lexical differences between AmE and BrE, there are also spelling differences which will be dealt with in the next paragraph.

British English, American English and Other Varieties of English

We are aware of the geographical varieties of English and we know that American English and British English are the most taught ones within programs of English language teaching all over the world. There are more than a few grammatical differences between BE and AE, but the outstanding divergences are in pronunciation, vocabulary and spelling. It is important to conform to one of the two standard varieties without mingling American and British elements at the same time. Though, it may be important, if you opt for one of the two standards, to know as many alternatives as you can in the other variety, just to be able to face with the language in most contexts possible.

We are not going to focus on pronunciation here as this is not a book of English phonology. We just aim to remind learners that there are some typical differences in the way the same words are pronounced in the two forms of the language. If you are familiar with the IPA (International Phonetic Alphabet), you will be able to see how to manage most differences.

As regards spelling we have indicated some of the most typical differences between the two varieties of English, but since exceptions do exist we recommend referencing a good dictionary for a more detailed treatment of the subject.

Spelling difference	British English	American English
-our, -or	Colour, honour, humour, labour	Color, honor, humor, labor
-re, -er	Caliber, centre, fibre, manoeuvre	Calibre, centrer, fiber, manoeuver
-ce, -se	Licence **(noun)**, license **(verb)**, practice **(noun)**, practise **(verb)**, defence, offence	License **(noun and verb)**, practice **(noun and verb)**, defense, offense
-xion, -ction	Connexion **(now rare)**	Connection
-ise, -ize	Organise, realise, recognise	Organize, realize, recognize
-yse, -yze	Analyse, catalyse	Analyze, catalyze
-ogue, -og	Catalogue, dialogue	Catalog, dialog
ae/oe, e/e	Anaemia, anaesthesia, oestrogen	Anemia, anesthesia, estrogen

The final consonant of an English word is sometimes doubled in both spelling systems when adding a suffix beginning with a vowel. Normally, this happens only when the word's final syllable is stressed and when it also ends with a single vowel followed by a single consonant. In BrE, however, a final -l is often doubled even when the final syllable is unstressed.

Doubled consonants	British English	American English
-ll (in BrE)	Cancelled, counsellor, cruellest, quarrelled, signalling, traveller	Canceled, counselor, cruelest, quarreled, signaling, traveler
-ll (in AmE)	Fulfil, enrol	Fulfill, enroll

BrE sometimes keeps silent e when adding suffixes. This does not happen in AmE.

Dropped E	British English	American English
-e (in BrE)	*Ageing, likeable, sizeable*	*Aging, likable, sizable*

Chapter 1
EMPLOYEES TEAM BUILDING

Pre-reading activity

Before reading the article below try to answer the following question:

Do you know the difference between an away day and a day off?

_____

_____

The expression away day is used in business English to describe a meeting, frequently of an entire department or sales team, which is not held on the premises, so away from the employees' regular office environment, usually for a whole day or a weekend. The purpose of an away day is to concentrate on a particular task without the participants being distracted by the duties that would normally involve them, if the meeting were held in the workplace. Instead, if you take a day off it means you have a day of holiday from work.

Now you should have a more precise idea of what an away day and a day off are, but before moving on to the reading activity have a look at the glossary below and become familiar with new words:

GLOSSARY

English word/phrase	English equivalent or definition
Beforehand	Previously
Contempt	Hatred, scorn
To run	To manage, to operate
The ebb and flow	Tidal movements; *fig.* fluctuations
To spice up	To make more exciting
To end up	To finish, to conclude, to culminate
Flip chart	a pad, with large sheets of paper that can be turned over, mounted on a stand and used to present figures, data, etc.
To simmer	To boil slowly; *fig.* to feel resentful
To boil over	To spill over when boiling; *fig.* to react angrily
To air	To express, to say
Bitching	A drag, a bore

Reading activity

The careerist: A successful away day

Done right, an away day can be an opportunity to plan strategy, deal with a variety of issues and build esprit de corps; done wrong it can be a waste of an expensive hotel.

How do you make an away day pay?

Should you plan?

"You need to have clear objectives," says Paul Kearns, a consultant on strategic corporate events. "Communicate what it is you're trying to achieve beforehand. If you don't have objectives you often won't produce anything." You should also ensure the right people attend. "If it is a serious meeting, you need the key players there," says Mr Kearns. "Important people can sometimes show contempt for these things."

How do I run the day?

"You need to recognise the ebb and flow of people's biorhythms," says Phil Anderson, client director at Ashridge Business School. "Don't have a PowerPoint presentation when people are feeling sleepy just after lunch. Spice it up and, if you are leading, get others to lead certain parts as people get bored of the same speaker.

"You need to think about breaks too; you often get insights over coffee when talking less formally."

The ideal day should combine serious business with fun and relaxation. "Games can work but they need to be appropriate to the organisation," says Mr Anderson. "Even with a strict business focus, it's good to get people to do something different." As away days tend to generate a lot of ideas, you should also evaluate as you go, so you don't end up with hundreds of flip charts at the end of the session.

What if there are disagreements?

Simmering resentments often boil over at such events. "Anticipate that there may be tensions," says Jane Clarke of business psychologists Nicholson McBride. "You might get an HR person to do a bit of research – what are the personality issues?"

If there are tensions, it's good to air them at the start, rather than letting them come out in the bar. "The rules of engagement need to be spelt out – and the difference between constructive and destructive criticism explained – or it can become a general bitching session," warns Mr Kearns. If things are difficult, it can make sense to have a professional facilitator.

How long should it be?

"Overnights are good," says Ms Clarke. "A lot of talking takes place in the bar or over dinner and you get a chance to work on both business strategy and individual relationships."

Mr Anderson points out that you should also remember that people have other commitments. "Don't make it too long. Arriving the night before and then finishing in the afternoon is good."

What about follow up?

"A lot of people leave feeling very motivated and then nothing happens," says Ms Clarke. This is often because the organiser attempts to do everything themselves afterwards. "A good way to ensure follow up happens is to give everyone something to do," says Mr Anderson. "That should happen before you leave. You also need agree a follow-up date to check which next steps have been taken and by whom."

Notes to the text

- English has always undergone the charm of French and especially in the past a lot of French words entered the English language. Despite the fact that today the process is quite the opposite a lot of French words are still used in English. Often they seem to be more elevated from a social point of view. In the article esprit de corps is used instead of team spirit or comradeship. Other words like these are au pair, bourgeois, bouquet, cliché, coup de foudre, crèche, entrepreneur, faux pas, joie de vivre, laissez-faire, malaise, nouveau riche, par excellence, raison d'etre, sang-froid, vis-à-vis and many others.

Being fairly new here I don't want to commit any faux pas

- The word corporate refers to corporation. The word corporation has a lot of synonyms in English that may allude to the various sizes or legal entities of a company: partnership, business, firm, company, enterprise, concern. The word business means company, and it is countable as in many businesses have announced closings or layoffs but it is uncountable when it refers to trade, the process of buying and selling, the activity of making money: business is business.

A going concern is the only kind of business banks lend money to, and suppliers extend credit to.

- The word run has various meanings. First it stands for go quickly, but it can also refer to run (a machine) = operate (a machine), or manage (a company, a shop, a department, etc.) that is be in charge of something. For ex. I have been running this shop since 2005.

- The word get is a sort of unique word in English which cannot be easily translated into other languages. The basic meaning of the verb is to obtain, to gain, to get hold of but it is also used with figurative meanings such as to buy, to persuade, to arrive, to understand, etc. For ex. In the sentence You might get an HR person to do a bit of research it means to persuade, convince.

- The verb get is also used to express a change of state or condition = to become. Common examples are get bored, get tired, get rich, get dirty, get drunk, get worried, get old. In some cases go, grow and turn can be used as well. Grow indicates a slow change whereas turn and go show a faster modification: I want to grow old with dignity – She turned/went pale and fell down

Post-reading activity 1 (Vocabulary)

Write the words below in the context they occur in the text:

English word/phrase	Context
Beforehand	
Contempt	
To run	
The ebb and flow	
To spice up	
To end up	
Flip chart	
To simmer	
To boil over	
To air	
Bitching	

Post-reading activity 2 (Comprehension)

Say whether these statements are true (T) or false (F):

1. Paul Kerns thinks that objectives have to be clear before arranging an away day

2. Important people in a company are always very interested in away days and similar events

3. A PowerPoint presentation is one of the best activities you can do just after lunch.

4. The ideal mix would be combining some fun and relaxation with serious business

5. An away day will probably not produce any useful ideas

6. Tensions and disagreements should come out at the end of the session

7. A professional facilitator might make things easier if they are difficult to manage

8. Corporate away days should not last more than a weekend

9. Most participants are very motivated after away days

10. A good way to ensure follow up happens is to give every participant a different task

Post-reading activity 3 (Speaking)

Do you think corporate away days are a good idea to increase staff productivity and encourage team spirit? Choose from the categories below the best team building activities and justify your ideas:

FOREST CHALLENGE

A spirited team race in the forest. Teams must stay on the right path while overcoming team challenges on the way.

TREASURE HUNT

A treasure hunt is a great method for teams to work together while having fun. GPS Treasure Hunts can be organised in a town, or in any other location of your choice.

SUMMIT OR BUST

Every team is given a survival rucksack and a map of Everest with a detailed route to the top, but there is no need for mountaineering experience on this trip because it is a tabletop game.

BUSHCRAFT CHALLENGE

A tough outdoor team building event survivors. Teams must build a shelter and make fire. They prepare a hot meal from what they find and signal to rescuers.

WINE TASTING

Perfect for raising spirits before an evening meal or to acknowledge your teams successes. Every team will need to work together to find out the origins and characteristics of wines from around the world.

WHO KILLED DR. X?

A new version of Cluedo played in detective teams with a huge game-board and dice. Teams move their counters around the board from room to room where clues or pieces of evidence are hidden.

Post-reading activity 4 (Writing)

Choose the proverb that would best fit the article about away days:

"Gettin' good players is easy. Gettin''em to play together is the hard part." – Casey Stengel, American baseball player

"If I could solve all the problems myself, I would." – Thomas Edison, Inventor

Post-reading activity 5 (Speaking)

You have been appointed by your company to arrange a meeting with employees to discuss the company goals and their roles in achieving them. Choose the best conference venue on the basis of the following:

200 participants expected

A two-day meeting is scheduled

Two thirds of the attendees come from London. The others come from Cambridge and Exeter

Clear and accurate budget is required

Remember that if you are to choose a venue for a meeting or conference there is more to consider than just the budget. When taking into account who is attending, you should ask the following about any potential location:

Does the location fit the company's image?

Will it appeal to the attendees?

Is the place easily reachable to those attending the meeting?

What is the seating capacity of the meeting?

Do they offer a projector, electronic whiteboard, stationery, and other useful equipment?

London Continental Hotel

Here are some significant information about London Continental:

- Centrally-located hotel
- Meeting room for up to 250 people
- Audio/visual equipment and free wireless internet
- Gym and swimming pool
- On-site dining at the chic Don Quijote restaurant
- Expensive room rates

Professional Meeting Centre (PMC)

Here are some significant information about the Professional Meeting Centre:

- Located in the city centre
- Maximum conference room up to 350 people

- Up-to-date equipment and free stationery
- Staffed reception
- Full service catering available
- Accommodation not available on-site

Four Roses Hotel

The following list provides some relevant information about Four Roses:

- Outside central London (70 km)
- Conference room capacity – 200 people
- Wireless internet connection available
- Garden and pool
- Fine food served, Italian cuisine
- Reasonable room prices
- Not easily accessible

Grammar revision

MODAL VERBS

A modal verb is a type of auxiliary verb that is used to indicate modality (likelihood, ability, permission, and obligation). This group of verbs share the following features:

They do not inflect except for few of them (present–past). They do not add -(e)s in the third-person singular.

They are defective: they are not used as infinitives or participles, as imperatives, nor as subjunctives.

They modify the meaning of the verbs they are associated with. This verb is generally a bare infinitive, but in some cases a modal verb can also be followed by the to-infinitive (as ought).

They have the same syntactic qualities as auxiliary verbs in English, so they can have subject–auxiliary inversion (in questions) and can be negated by adding not after the verb.

Modal verb	Function	Example
Can	Ability Permissibility Possible circumstance	I can write an effective cv You can smoke here Incentives can help salespeople to seal a deal
Could	Past tense of 'can' Conditional form of 'can'	I could speak some French when I was younger I could help you if you asked me
May	Permissibility Possible circumstance	You may not attend the meeting The meeting may finish later than scheduled
Might	Possible circumstance	The meeting might finish later than scheduled

Should	Expected or recommended behavior or circumstance	You should attend meetings if you want to be updated
Must	Expresses obligation or necessity from the speaker's point of view. The negative expresses prohibition	You must attend today's meeting You mustn't touch anything on my desk
Shall	In questions (in the 1st person) to ask for advice or confirmation of a suggestion	Shall we go the meeting?
Have to	Expresses obligation or necessity coming from rules, norms and outside regulations. The negative *don't have to* expresses lack of necessity. *Have to* also expresses other forms in which *must* is defective (past, present perfect,...)	In the company managers have to attend monthly meetings You don't have to attend the meeting if you don't like to. It's not obligatory. Yesterday I had to go to the bank

Will	It often expresses futurity, but as a modal expresses habitual aspect, strong probability in the present and orders	The meeting will be held on Tuesday He will preside over the meeting That will be Mr Smith at the door You will apologise right now!
Would	Conditional form of verbs and habitual aspect in the past (similar to *used to*)	In Florence I would have an early wake-up and I would drive to work
Ought to	Similar to *should* but is followed by the to infinitive	You ought to attend meetings if you want to be updated
Had better	Similar meaning to *should* and *ought*	Hadn't we better attend the meeting?
Need	As a modal it is usually limited to questions and negative forms and means obligation (similar to *must*). The negative *needn't* + bare infinitive means lack of necessity (as *don't have to*)	Need I go on? You needn't attend the meeting if you don't like to. It's not obligatory.

Be able to is not a modal verb. It is simply the verb be followed by the adjective able plus the infinitive. It is used to express ability in all tenses but it is mostly used when can and could cannot be used. In addition to it, if could is used for general ability in the past, be able to is used to refer to ability on one occasion:

I have never been able to swim   I will be able to speak good English one day

In Susan's case the manager was able to make use of her relationship with them in order to avoid problems

Grammar exercises

1. Choose the right modal verb:

1. You seem to be late for work. _____ I help you?

Would

Had better

Shall

2. I don't have my mobile today. _____ I borrow yours?

Must

Could

Shall

3. That man is very unkind. He _____ be so impolite to customers.

shouldn't

might not

had better

4. Tomorrow I'm leaving for Milan very early in the morning. I _____ to go to bed.

Should

Ought

could

5. The only thing I am afraid of is, that the directors _____ decide to sell the company too.

Might

Can

Would

6. Paul is over two hours late. He _____ missed the bus again.

Could

need have

could have

7. You _____ disclose any information about the customer to people.

don't have to

mustn't

needn't

8. You _____ sell your shares before the price goes down quickly.

Ought

had better

shall

2. Replace the verb in bold with another verb without changing the meaning of the sentence:

1. I **got** a necklace for Christmas from my family

2. I think I'll **get** him a tablet for his birthday

3. How do you **get** to school? By bus or on foot?

4. It's **getting** dark! We'd better go home now.

5. If my English **gets better** I might try to write a story

6. I **got** my boss to give me a pay rise

7. I guess he didn't **get** what I said

Chapter 2
EMPLOYEES STAFF MOTIVATION

Pre-reading activity

Before reading the article below, try to answer the following question. If you cannot answer look the word up in a dictionary:

What is motivation?

How do you get motivated to do something?

What does motivation have to do with studying?

A person without goals in life has the highest chance of becoming demotivated. Do you agree/why?

Now you should have a more precise idea of what motivation is, so move on to the reading activity. If you do not understand some words you can use the glossary at the end of the article, which will help you get familiar with some of the words you will encounter in the text:

Reading activity

4 Demotivators That Will Cost You

Keeping everyone on your team focused and motivated is not easy, especially if you fall into one or more of these common traps.

If you feel that people are the most valuable asset at a business--and we certainly do--it's important to keep everyone motivated and sailing towards the same port. Recently, we wrote about three things business leaders can do to motivate their team. Equally important is what you should avoid doing.

1. Don't motivate solely on salary.

Salary might be why someone leaves your firm, but it won't be why they stay. Paying a competitive salary is table stakes, but it's an extrinsic motivator. To tap into people's intrinsic motivation, focus on creating an environment that encourages everyone to take ownership, communicate the purpose behind the work, and maintain a positive environment that encourages the open exchange of ideas. Cash-based incentives can help to deliver results in the short term, but long-term success requires a higher form of motivation.

2. Don't multitask when you're meeting with people.

There's no quicker way to undermine the importance of your employees than by actively engaging with your cell phone, laptop, or tablet during meetings. By not giving your full attention to the team, they will feel second rate and less motivated. Leaders must set the tone that everyone's time is valuable and that people deserve full attention when discussing business issues.

3. Don't deliver mixed messages.

Delivering different messages to different people is an easy trap to fall into, but it's exactly that--a trap. Communicate consistently to increase efficiency and give people the complete confidence that the game of telephone won't be played in your organization. While using different styles with different audiences is a critical part of being a successful leader, don't confuse this with tweaking the actual content of your message because you perceive different parties might want to hear different things.

4. Don't stifle creativity by shooting down 'dumb' ideas.

Creating and sharing ideas is part of a healthy work environment. By quickly shooting down people's ideas, you're likely to stifle creativity. Next time you're faced with an idea you're not initially fond of--and there will be lots of them--try using this idea as the launching point for a broader brainstorming session. Encourage the creation of long lists of potential solutions to a problem. Ideas one through 10 on the brainstorm list are likely to be straightforward, but by the time you get to idea 25, 52, or 78, you might really experience a breakthrough. New ideas to solve problems are the essence of successful companies, so be sure to create a culture where ideas are treasured, not trashed. Avoiding these common traps will help business leaders create lasting motivation for their teams.

From www.inc.com – by Karl Stark and Bill Stewart

Mansueto Ventures LLC. All rights reserved – Reproduced with permission

GLOSSARY

English word or phrase	English equivalent or definition
To sail	To travel by sailboat; *fig.* move quickly and easily
Solely	Exclusively; completely
Table stakes	a stake that a player places on the table at the start of a poker game as the amount he/she is willing to bet; *fig.* first priority
To tap into	To gain access to, to take advantage of
Second rate	Not the best, inferior
Consistently	Constantly, regularly
Game of telephone	Chinese whispers or *fig.* any situation where information is passed on in turn by a number of people, often becoming distorted in the process
To tweak	To modify slightly, to alter
To stifle	To suppress, to suffocate
To shoot down	To defeat or disprove
Straightforward	Simple, uncomplicated; direct
Breakthrough	Major progress or advance, discovery
To treasure	To appreciate
To trash	To criticize, to destroy

Notes to the text

- In the article it is evident how words and expressions can be used metaphorically. In some cases metaphors are culture related so they do not make sense to a foreigner, but in some cases metaphors are universal or also common in other languages and cultures. The expression to fall into a trap is obviously metaphorical and means to be deceived into acting or thinking something which turned out to be different. Also the expression sailing towards the same port means to have common targets and so the meaning is figurative.

- The word multitask was first used in computing and then applied to people's attitude to perform many things simultaneously

Multitasking can reduce productivity dramatically

- Some words are polysemous, that is they can have various meanings. The word straightforward may refer to a person's character if they are frank, honest and direct, but it is also used to say that something is easy, uncomplicated. The word consistent means either regular and habitual but also free from contradiction.

Straightforwardness is valued in some societies more than in others

Post-reading activity 1 (Writing)

In the article "4 demotivators that will cost you", the author focuses on what business leaders should avoid doing in order not to demotivate staff. Can you summarise his reasons and say why they may have negative effects on employees. Do you agree with the author?

BEST AVOIDED	**NEGATIVE EFFECTS LIKELY TO OCCUR**	**AGREE/DISAGREE - WHY**
1._____		

2. _____		
3. _____		
4. _____		

Post-reading activity 2 (Comprehension)

Test your motivation skills. Are you motivated to achieve your goals? This test was prepared by Mind Tools. It is a company founded by James Manktelow in 1996, focused on teaching the essential skills for an excellent career.

How self-motivated are you?

Instructions: For each statement, put a tick in the column that best describes you. Answer questions as you actually are and when you have finished, you can calculate your score by following the directions provided on the website:

1. I'm unsure of my ability to achieve the goals I set for myself.

   Not at all   Rarely   Sometimes   Often   Very often

2. When working on my goals, I put in maximum effort and work even harder if I've suffered a setback.

   Not at all   Rarely   Sometimes   Often   Very often

3. I regularly set goals and objectives to achieve my vision for my life.

   Not at all   Rarely   Sometimes   Often   Very often

4. I think positively about setting goals and making sure my needs are met.

   Not at all   Rarely   Sometimes   Often   Very often

5. I use rewards (and consequences) to keep myself focused. For example, if I finish my report on time, I allow myself to take a coffee break.

   Not at all   Rarely   Sometimes   Often   Very often

6. I believe that if I work hard and apply my abilities and talents, I will be successful.

   Not at all   Rarely   Sometimes   Often   Very often

7. I worry about deadlines and getting things done, which causes stress and anxiety.

   Not at all   Rarely   Sometimes   Often   Very often

8. When an unexpected event threatens or jeopardizes my goal, I can tend to walk away, set a different goal, and move in a new direction.

    Not at all   Rarely   Sometimes   Often   Very often

9. My biggest reward after completing something is the satisfaction of knowing I've done a good job.

    Not at all   Rarely   Sometimes   Often   Very often

10. I tend to do the minimum amount of work necessary to keep my boss and my team satisfied.

    Not at all   Rarely   Sometimes   Often   Very often

11. I tend to worry about why I won't reach my goals, and I often focus on why something probably won't work.

    Not at all   Rarely   Sometimes   Often   Very often

12. I create a vivid and powerful vision of my future success before embarking on a new goal.

    Not at all   Rarely   Sometimes   Often   Very often

Post-reading activity 3 (Speaking)

Now, working in pairs, think about the result you have obtained and say whether you agree or not with it. Then, write down a list of things you could do to improve your motivating skills. After that, in a group do the same thing with your partners, by giving them advice and accepting their suggestions.

Supplementary activity 1 (Speaking)

If you were a manager, which of the following items would you consider to be a critical part of good staff motivation?

Be familiar with your staff – provide the employees some benefits – acknowledge your employees on their achievement – give your staff learning opportunities – smile often – ensure effective communication – flexibility – others

Vocabulary activity

Match the adjectives on the left with the definitions on the right. Then match the same adjectives with the nouns in A. that collocate with them:

Multifaceted   designed for many uses

Multipurpose	sequential, graduated
Multistep	expressed in several languages, or having the ability to use many
Multicultural	containing multiple cultures
Multilingual	having many aspects
Multiage	having several layers, strata or levels
Multiparty	involving different age groups
Multilayer(ed)	involving several political parties

A. country – vehicle – cake – classroom – method – issue – government – environment

Post-reading activity 4 (Writing)

Choose the proverb that would best fit the article about motivation:

"Always treat your employees exactly as you want them to treat your best customers." – Stephen R. Covey, Author

"Motivation is what gets you started. Habit is what keeps you going." – Jim Rohn, Entrepreneur, Speaker

Grammar revision

IMPERATIVE

The imperative form is used to give instructions or orders. It is also common in written instructions. When you use the imperative, you should be careful because it might be considered impolite under some circumstances, so use please if you are making a request:

Positive	Negative
Base Form of Verb	Do + Not (Don't) + Base Form of Verb
Focus on creating an encouraging environment	Don't motivate solely on salary
Communicate the purpose behind the work	Don't multitask when you're meeting with people
Encourage the creation of long lists	Don't deliver mixed messages

The imperative is generally used for the you subject, but you can also use "let's" before the verb if you want to include yourself in the imperative (proposals, warnings, etc.):

Let us (Let's) + Base Form of Verb   Let us (Let's) + not + Base Form of Verb

Let's involve all the team in the matter   Let's not involve all the team in the matter

ADVERBS OF FREQUENCY

Adverbs of frequency tell us about the frequency of an action. In Post-reading activity 2 the test needed an answer such as rarely, sometimes, often, etc. These are examples of frequency adverbs and the following is a chart explaining how to use them:

Never   Rarely/seldom   Occasionally   Sometimes   Often   Always

The position of these adverbs in a sentence is: subject + adverb of frequency + verb such as we have in:

I never go to meetings on Saturdays

She often goes to work by car

With auxiliary verbs (do, be, have, can, ...) they follow the auxiliary such as we have in:

I don't often study English

We are not always very punctual

Jim is never late at work

Often, usually, sometimes and occasionally can go at the beginning of a sentence

Grammar exercises

1. Put the following sentences into the correct form of the imperative (positive or negative) based on what is stated in the article:

Ex. Creating and sharing ideas in your work environment = Create and share ideas in ...

1. Shooting down people's ideas

    =

2. Avoiding these common traps

   =

3. Paying a competitive salary

   =

4. To undermine the importance of your employees

   =

5. Engaging with your cell phone, laptop, or tablet during meetings.

   =

6. Delivering different messages to different people

   =

2. Put the following sentences into the imperative form using let's do/go/eat... or let's not do/go/eat...

1. It's 1 pm and you didn't have breakfast in the morning. You are very hungry. What do you say to your friends? (Use have)

2. You and your colleagues have just finished dinner at a cheesy restaurant and are looking forward to leaving. What do you say? (Use pay)

3. Paul has just come at the party. You know that he has broken up with Sarah so what do you advise your friends not to do? (Use talk about)

4. Pamela caught a fever and she is resting now. You arrive at home with Mary. What do you say? (Use make a noise)

5. The speaker has arrived at the conference at last! You think everything is ready to start. What do you say? (Use get started)

3. Rewrite each sentence using the adverb of frequency in brackets in its correct position:

1. How often do you go to the cinema? I go to the cinema (seldom)

2. We spend Christmas with friends (usually)

3. Mary is late because she hates keeping people waiting (never)

4. I take sugar in my tea (sometimes)

5. My uncle goes for a stroll on Sundays (always)

6. I can say what I think or I am fired (never)

7. I am very busy but I will try to do my best (always)

Chapter 3
COMPANIES START-UPS

Pre-reading activity

Before reading the article below, try to answer the following question. If you cannot answer look the word up in a dictionary:

What is a start-up?

_____

_____

Now you should have a more precise idea of what a start-up is, so move on to the reading activity. In order to make your reading easier, the article has been divided into paragraphs. Read each paragraph twice. If you do not understand some words you can use the glossary at the end of the article.

Reading activity A

My Week: Andy Shovel of Burgers and Stuff

With his business partner Peter Sharman, Shovel devised a business plan for a new upmarket burger delivery chain. Funding from investors has just landed.

Par. 1

With the first tranche of our investors' funding having only just landed, and a launch date of March 2013, there is still a lot to do to fine tune the operation. This week we've just finished off the process of finding a branding agency to mastermind our image; we've been on the new premises with builders and shop fitters to get quotes; we've been seeing packaging producers to refine the design of our burger box; we've met a scooter supplier to choose what bikes we want our delivery men on; we've even met a pickles specialist to help us choose the best toppings for our burgers. And that's all in the one week.

Par. 2

The idea came after I sold off some of my previous start-up, Recruitment Squared, because I wasn't enjoying the office environment. I wanted to do something more fun. Originally the idea was to start an American-style healthy fast-food bar in the City of London, but I went off of this in favour of the burger delivery concept. That was when I met my now business partner Peter Sharman and we began working through all the challenges. One of the main hurdles has been packaging: maintaining the quality and the 'structure' of a prepared burger whilst having to carry it in a box on a scooter is tough. We've even got a patent on our box design because of the way it protects the burger from flipping or getting soggy, but still manages to keep it hot.

Par. 3

We started by meeting with lots of industry insiders – owner/operators of fast food businesses. Then we spent three months writing a business plan with which to approach investors. We needed £250,000, and we've just secured this amount from some pizza delivery moguls. There are still a few obstacles to get past: the brand needs to be improved and consolidated – we may even change the name of the company before the launch. There's more recipe development to be done, and we're going to visit the States on a New York, Los Angeles and Florida tour, trying out American diners and burger joints to see if there's anything we can learn.

Par. 4

The best thing about the job so far is that there is such a wide variety of things we have to do. We'll be going through financial issues one day, tasting pickles the next day, and talking to builders about refurb options the day after that. But, easily the hardest thing about the process so far has been finding the best meat recipe in the UK. We've spent about seven months eating burgers four or five times a week, made from meats from all different corners of the globe. Before this, we had only amateur, rudimentary knowledge about how a good burger should taste.

Par. 5

So the first store opens in March, and we're both going to be in the kitchen, flipping burgers and doing deliveries. Over the course of that year, if things go to plan, we'll be hoping quickly to expand and open more sites: perhaps as many as three will be open by the end of the first year. The experience of pitching to investors was fun and luckily it went off without incident. We didn't meet anyone who seemed completely disinterested in our idea. Incidentally, our first pitch and burger tasting was to Pret A Manger founder Julian Metcalfe. We prepared some burgers and went over to his

Knightsbridge house on a scooter, but hit an enormous pothole in the road on the way. This was the first time we had tested the packaging and we were extremely worried the burger would be ruined by the time we got there. When we did arrive, Metcalfe said he would make it harder by telling us not to open the packaging for at least ten minutes. Luckily, our box design had worked and the burger was intact.

Par. 6

I am most looking forward to having a consumer brand for the first time. At the end of year one we expect to be breaking even or profitable. It's a long-term plan though, as we would like to develop a lot of sites, so a lot of money will be spent growing as well. From our experience so far on this project, my advice to any budding entrepreneurs is: if you have an idea that you're serious about, arrange to meet owner-operators of leading businesses in that sector. You'll learn loads and make good contacts. I'm 25 years old, but people aren't as intimidating as you think towards a young person starting a business.

Notes to the text

- The adjective upmarket means expensive, luxury, exclusive and its opposite downmarket means for low income consumers, second rate, low quality. The particles up and down are commonly used as prefixes to make adjectives, nouns and verbs. They usually have to do with movement towards an elevated point, higher rank or vice versa. Some examples are uptown/downtown, upload/download, upgrade/downgrade, uprate/downrate.

I upgraded my internet to high speed from regular, but when I download songs it still loads at the same slow speed

- Whilst can be a synonym of while but in case of whilst + gerund it means though (it. pur, pur di).

There was a show whilst we were eating

I had to pay for the meal whilst not receiving the entire meal.

- A patent is a document granting the legal right to make or use an invention for a period of time (it. brevetto). It sounds similar to it. patente which is licence or permit.

So you have an idea and want to get a patent?

If my learner's driving licence is lost, do I need to apply for a duplicate to attend the driving test?

- When things go to plan they go the right way or according to schedule. An incident is an unpleasant and unusual event whereas an accident is an unexpected and unintentional event with negative effects.

The accident happened because the driver in front stopped so suddenly

Under different circumstances, this incident could have resulted in damage

- Loads is an informal way to say a lot, a large amount

You'll learn loads and make good contacts

You'll learn a lot and make good contacts

GLOSSARY

English word/phrase	English equivalent or definition
Upmarket	Expensive, luxury, exclusive
Burger delivery chain	A group of restaurants offering the carrying of food to your home or office
To fine tune	To refine, to adjust precisely, to set
To mastermind	To plan, to organize, to plot, to project
Premises	Especially a place of business
Shop fitter	Someone that makes furniture and equipment for stores and puts it in place
Quotes	Estimates, price, offer
Pickle	Any vegetable preserved in vinegar
To go off	To lose one's liking for sth.
Hurdle	Obstacle, difficulty
To flip	To turn over
To get soggy	To get soaked, to become soft
Mogul	Magnate, tycoon
Recipe	List of ingredients and instructions for making sth., (food)
Burger joints	Any restaurant that primarily serves burgers and fries
To refurb = refurbish	To renovate, to reequip, to restore
To pitch	To aim to sell
Pothole	Cave or hole
Budding	Developing, promising

Post-reading activity A 1

Answer the following questions about the article:

Refer to par. 1 of the article

When did the first tranche of money arrive?

How far is the launch date from now?

Have they met the branding agency yet? And why?

Why have builders and shop fitters been to the shop?

Why have they met their packaging producers?

Do they have an idea about how to choose the best toppings for their burgers?

Refer to par. 2 of the article

Why did one of the men sell off his previous company?

What was the original idea of his start-up?

Who is his current business partner?

Why is packaging one of the main hurdles?

Do their burgers risk flipping or getting soggy?

Refer to par. 3 of the article

Did they create a business plan? And why?

How did they raise the money they needed?

Have they named their shop yet?

Why are they planning to go the US?

Refer to par. 4 of the article

What is likely to happen in the next few days?

What is the hardest thing they have been doing so far?

Do they have an amateur knowledge of burgers?

Refer to par. 5 of the article

How many burger joints are they going to open if things go to plan?

Who was their first pitch and burger tasting?

Why were they afraid of his judgment?

Refer to par. 6 of the article

What expectations of profit do they have for the end of the year?

What kind of advice do they have for young entrepreneurs?

Post-reading activity A 2 (Writing)

Read the article again and summarise what it is about. Use paragraphs in the article to help you.

Post-reading activity A 3 (Speaking)

Say whether Shovel and Sharman's new business is likely to be successful. Then you should take into consideration all the information provided in the article and describe the pros and cons of starting up that business in your area. If you think this start-up would not be successful in your country say why and give alternative ideas on how to start a business in the food industry.

Post-reading activity A 4 (Writing)

Choose the proverb that would best fit the article about Shovel and Sharman's new business experience:

"A pessimist sees the difficulty in every opportunity; an optimist sees the opportunity in every difficulty." – Winston Churchill, British politician

"If your ship doesn't come in, swim out to meet it." – Jonathan Winters, American actor

Supplementary activity 1 (Listening)

An interview to Andy Shovel and Peter Sherman, the founders of Burgers and stuff is available on YouTube. Watch the video and you will find further information about their start-up.

Supplementary activity 2 (Research)

When someone starts a business, he/she must decide what form of business entity to set up. The form of business you choose will determine the type of income tax return form you have to file. Most businesses in the UK are sole traders, limited companies and business partnerships (AmE terms may vary considerably from BrE). The choice of the form of business is connected with legal and tax considerations. What would be the best business structure for an activity such as burger delivery based on the information given below?

Structure	Pros	Cons
Sole trader	Low cost, easy to set up Full control retained Very little financial reporting	Full liability for debt Pay more in tax Lacks credibility in market
Partnership	The above, but with more heads	The above, affecting all partners

	More potential to raise finance	Can be messy to wind up
Limited company	Less personal financial exposure	Administrative and regulatory demands heavier
	Favourable tax regime	Annual accounts and financial reports must be placed in public domain
	Ability to work for corporate clients	

Vocabulary activity 1

Match the words below with the correct definition:

Upbringing

Down-market

Upturn

Uploading

Updated

Downtime

Downgraded

Downsizing

Downtown

Upsurge

Uptake

Downward(s)

1. He found it humiliating to have to buy _____ products

2. Can you tell me when this webpage was last _____?

3. With a free account, you can _____ an unlimited number of photos

4. _____ is a term for reducing the number of employees in a company

5. Are there parental responsibilities in the _____ of children?

6. There has been an _____ of international interest in ethnic conflicts

7. I live in the _____ area.

8. The company's shares were _____ today by two notches

9. I wouldn't be so hopeful for a quick _____ in the economy.

10. Unscheduled factory _____ decreases company profits

11. It helps to reduce the fat _____ and the absorption of cholesterol

12. _____ means going down from a higher to a lower level, position, etc.

Vocabulary activity 2

Tax related words

The form of business you operate determines what taxes you must pay. The following are some words related to taxation. Match them with the correct definition:

Taxpayer

Internal Revenue Service, IRS

Tax evasion

To bribe

Tax avoidance

Fiscal watchdog

Amnesty

Property tax

Income tax

Fraud

1. the bureau of the Treasury Department responsible for tax collections

2. a personal tax levied on annual income

3. make illegal payments to in exchange for favours

4. Someone who pays taxes

5. something intended to deceive; deliberate trickery, intended to gain an advantage

6. a warrant granting release from punishment for an offense

7. a capital tax on property imposed by municipalities based on the estimated value of the property

8. a fiscal guardian or defender against theft or illegal practices or waste

9. illegal practice where people and corporations intentionally avoid paying their true tax liability

10. the minimization of tax liability by lawful methods

Supplementary activity 3 (Speaking)

Discuss with the class the meaning of the data in the chart below. Are you surprised by the results?

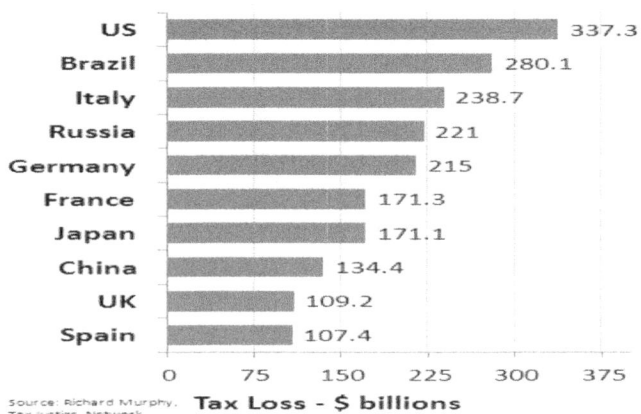

Pre-reading activity B

Write down the meaning:

To be a good fit	
Fee	
Screening	
To meet the requirements	
Managing director	
To forward	
Due diligence	

Eventually	
Elevator pitch	
Q&A	
To be willing	
In depth	
Commitment	
Special Purpose Vehicle	
Board (of Directors)	
Advisory Board	

Reading activity B

Read the presentation below. It is about a Business Angel Group in Italy called Italian Angels for Growth.. Business angels are experienced investors who provide capital for start-up companies. After reading, try to answer the questions.

HOW WE WORK

IAG developed a structured and thorough process to select the best opportunities to be presented to its members

SCREENING PROCESS

a. The Company is encouraged to read carefully the website before going through the application process to be sure there is a good fit between the company's focus and members' interests.

b. Complete the online application form.

c. Once you go through the application process, you will be asked to pay a €50 application fee. This fee is non-refundable, so it is important to check the website and determine if there's a fit between your company and our investment focus.

d. Your application will be complete once you have finalized all of the steps outlined above. Your application will not be reviewed until it's fully completed.

e. e. Our members are free to identify companies in which they are interested, therefore is no guarantee that your company will be invited to give an investment presentation.

1. FIRST EVALUATION

When IAG receives a project, the first phase is called Pre-screening. This consists of a preliminary analysis of the business plan in order to verify that the essential requirements are met for IAG members to consider it as an investment (i.e. owned and defensible innovation over time, high growth potential and relevance to the other elements of the investment focus).

The opportunities are pre-selected by a Managing Director, with the cooperation of our internal team. If the proposal successfully goes through this phase, it will then proceed to the second phase called Screening. Only the proposals most relevant to the investment focus will be forwarded to the members, and will then have access to the second phase of screening.

2. SCREENING

In this phase a group of 2 – 5 members of IAG with knowledge of the industrial sector will be created. The group will analyze the business plan and further documentation sent by the entrepreneur in a confidential procedure. If there is a positive answer from the group, a meeting will be scheduled with the team or owner of the plan, to personally meet the IAG members. This is one of the most important phases of the process of selection, as the entrepreneur and team are one of the most relevant variables in the investment decision-making process. After the meeting, the screening group will express their opinions regarding technology, and business plan to the team, and on the presentation qualities it has to meet in order to be handed to the Screening Committee. If the feedback is positive, then the plan will be taken forward.

3. THE SCREENING COMMITTEE

The committee (composed of 6 IAG members) meets once every two months to select the best 2/4 projects, which will then be presented to all members in the Company Presentation meeting. One or more members of the screening group will volunteer to be an internal sponsor for the opportunity, prior to its presentation, and to follow the Due Diligence and eventually, the negotiation of terms and conditions of the investments, in case the members appreciate the initiative.

4. COMPANY PRESENTATION MEETING

The company presentation meetings take place every 2 months and a half approximately, (totaling 5 per year). In these occasions the entrepreneurs of the selected projects, are invited to present their initiative and have 15 minutes to do so. At the end of the elevator pitch a session of Q&A of 15 minutes will follow, and after that a closed door discussion session between the IAG members. At the end of the day, every member individually expresses his/her opinion on the presented companies and indicates the desired amount that they are willing to invest subject to Due Diligence.

5. DUE DILIGENCE

If the opportunity presented by the members, has collected enough commitment, the Sponsor (from this moment called the Deal Champion), starts the Due Diligence phase, during which in depth checks will be undertaken on the technology, on the business and the legal aspects. If no problems or obstacles are found, the Due Diligence will normally last for 2 months.

6. INVESTMENT

Once the Due diligence is over, the members are invited to confirm or withdraw their commitment announced after the company presentation. The investment members of every single investment will proceed as a group to drafting the contracts, the special purpose vehicle used for the investment and the "closing".

7. POST-INVESTMENT INVOLVEMENT

The IAG members tend to have an active role in the companies they invest in. Often the Deal Champion will sit in the Board or be part of the Advisory Board of the companies in the portfolio. The other members of the consortium of investment are always available in bringing their value, in terms of contacts as well as industrial expertise.

Post-reading activity B 1 (Writing)

Answer the following questions about the article:

1. What does IAG mean?
2. What does the company do?
3. How many steps are involved in screening process?
4. Why is the pre-screening phase necessary?
5. What kind of proposals are most likely to be accepted?
6. How many people are in the Screening committee?
7. When can the entrepreneur of the selected project present his/her initiative to the company?
8. Why is the Due Diligence so important?
9. What comes after the Due Diligence phase?
10. What happens in the post-investment phase?

Post-reading activity B 2 (Speaking)

Imagine you are an angel investor. Which of the following proposals would you take into account? Which ones would you eliminate?

A. Smart shirt helps wearers keep track of their mental and physical wellbeing

- Embedded with sensors able to detect and track the wearer's emotional state
- Monitor heart rate and breathing
- Information could be shared socially for fun or to keep a check on friends and family members' health

B. Biodegradable cigarette filter helps clear streets of discarded butts

- Cigarette filter made of organic material that biodegrades in weeks
- Improves the quality of the smoke by reducing the number of synthetic chemicals
- Help reduce the impact smokers have on the environment

C. Airport vending machine 'restaurant' offers gourmet menu

- A sit-down vending machine restaurant
- Gourmet food 24 hours a day
- Select from the menu and delivered instantly

D. Printing methods work on any surface

- High quality printing on any surface
- Place messages in uncommon locations
- Open up interesting new art forms

Grammar revision

PAST SIMPLE

I CLEANED

(Used for activities or events completed in the past, either understood or indicate by a time expression)

I wanted to do something more fun

We started by meeting with lots of industry insiders

Then we spent three months writing a business plan

Subject + past form of the verb

Did + subject + bare infinitive

Subject + did + not + bare infinitive

_ _ ___I_____I_____ _ _

Now

PAST CONTINUOUS

I WAS CLEANING

(Used for temporary actions or events that were taking place at a particular time in the past)

I wasn't enjoying the office environment

Yesterday at 11 pm I was still doing deliveries

While we were delivering burgers we hit a big pothole in the road

Subject + was/were + -ing form

Was/were + subject + -ing form

Subject + Was/were + not + -ing form

_ _ __IIIIII_____I____ _ _

Now

PRESENT PERFECT SIMPLE

I HAVE CLEANED

(Used for a complete past action connected with the present. The result or the effect of the action is visible now. It is used with already, just, yet, never, ever. It is also used to refer to a period of time that hasn't finished yet)

This week we've just finished off the process of...

We've been on the new premises with builders and ...

We've met a scooter supplier

Subject + have/has + past participle

Have/has + subject + past participle

Subject + have/has + not + past participle

Now

PRESENT PERFECT CONTINUOUS

I HAVE BEEN CLEANING

(Used for actions that started in the past which are still in progress or just finished.

Emphasis is on the activity. It is also used with for /since to say how long an action

has been going on)

We've been seeing packaging producers this week

We have been working together since few weeks

Why are you so late? I've been waiting for over an hour

Subject + have/has + been + ing form

Have/has + subject + been + ing form

Subject + have/has + not + been + ing form

Now

Grammar exercises

1. Put the following sentences in the correct form of the present perfect simple:

1. We (finish off)_____ the process of finding a branding agency.

2. We (not/be)_____ on the new premises yet.

3. We (not/meet)_____ a scooter supplier yet.

4. We (spend)_____ about seven months eating burgers four or five times a week.

5. Packaging (be)_____one of the main hurdles.

2. Put the following sentences in the correct form of the past simple:

1. The idea (come)_____ after I (sell off)_____ some of my previous start-up.

2. I (want)_____ to do something more fun.

3. Peter Sharman and I (begin)_____ working through all the challenges.

4. We (spend)_____ three months writing a business plan.

5. We (not/meet)_____ anyone who seemed completely disinterested in our idea.

6. We (prepare)_____ some burgers and (go)_____ over to his house on a scooter.

7. We (hit)_____ an enormous pothole in the road on the way.

8. So we (be)_____ extremely worried the burger would be ruined.

3. Choose the correct tense (present perfect/past simple) for each of the following sentences:

1. The first tranche of our investors' funding has landed/landed yesterday.

2. We have just secured/just secured financial support from some pizza delivery moguls.

3. This week we found/have found a branding agency that will mastermind our image.

4. Last Tuesday we have met/met a scooter supplier.

5. The idea came/has come after I have sold off/sold off some of my previous start-up.

6. We spent/have spent about seven months eating burgers four or five times a week so far.

7. Before tasting meat from all over the world, we had/have had only amateur knowledge about how a good burger should taste.

8. When we arrived/have arrived there, Julian Metcalfe hasn't opened/didn't open the packaging for at least ten minutes.

9. By meeting other entrepreneurs I learned/have learned a lot in the last few months.

10. Last September, in our tour through the States we have tried out/tried out a lot of American diners.

4. Put the following sentences in the correct form of the present perfect continuous:

1. We (meet)_____ scooter suppliers _____ over two weeks

2. We (write) _____ our business plan _____ three months

3. Where is Andy? I think he is on the phone with the pickles specialist. They (talk)_____ since 2 o' clock

4. Peter (cook)_____ for three hours

5. I (eat) _____ burgers for seven months

Remember that verbs may be divided into action and state verbs. Action verbs describe action we take and facts. State verbs describe conditions, states of being, likes or dislikes, opinions. They cannot be used in the –ing form. Here is a short list of state verbs:

Agree, approve of, believe, belong to, consider (hold an opinion), consist of, contain, cost, depend, disagree, gather (understand), hate, have (own), know, like, loathe, love, mean, own, need, possess, prefer, realize, regret, remember, resemble, suppose, think (hold an opinion), understand, want, wish, etc.

Ex. I have known Mary for ten years

5. Put the following sentences in the correct form of the past continuous. If it is not possible use the past simple:

1. When the consultant arrived, I (read)_____ a leaflet in the waiting room

2. While we (talk) _____ to builders about refurb options, we received a strange phone call

3. When the meeting started nobody (know)_____ some investors had decided to fund our business

4. Despite my best efforts to explain the project I realised they (not/understand) what I (say)_____ to them

5. Yesterday at 10.30 pm I (deliver) still _____ some pizzas.

6. When the French meat supplier called us we (deal)_____ with other issues

Chapter 4
ACTIVITIES MARKETING

Pre-reading activity A

Before reading the article below answer the following question:

What is marketing?

_____

_____

According to the Oxford English Dictionary the word marketing refers to "the action or business of bringing or sending a product or commodity to market; (now chiefly, Business) the action, business, or process of promoting and selling a product, etc., including market research, advertising, and distribution".

The marketing mix is a business method employed in marketing and by marketing professionals. It is important as it is the combination of the elements needed to determine a product or brand's offering, and it is often associated with the four Ps: price, product, promotion, and place. Can you explain how to use these factors to achieve your profit potential?

Now you should have a more precise idea of what marketing is, so move on to the pre-reading activity. Match the words and phrases on the left with the appropriate definition on the right:

Reading activity A (Vocabulary)

Before reading the article below focus on understanding new vocabulary. Match the words on the left to their definitions on the right:

1. Sticks with ence to   a. a kind of march, rigid adherence to procedure

2. Run of the mill   b. connect, link

3. Tie   c. to put on display, to present

4. Sleight of hand   d. ordinary

5. Lock step   e. to gain useful access to sthg.

6. To showcase   f. chance, future possibility

7. To tap   g. magic trick, quick fingers

8. Prospects   h. remains loyal to

Where Has All The Good Marketing Gone?

What You Can Learn From Top Marketers

I don't know about you, but I feel like there is a scarcity of good marketing today. What do I mean "good marketing?" You know the kind of marketing that sticks with you and drives you to take action. The only marketing that has really moved me in the last couple of years has been from Apple. How do I know? I own 3 ipods.

You might be thinking to yourself that it's more the product that drives behavior than the marketing, and when it comes to the ipod I don't necessarily disagree. However, I would argue that in some ways, the marketing has to be even better than it does with your run of the mill product.

Apple has maintained a certain level of success with their marketing and now that marketing must not only tie together with previous marketing campaigns, but convince current customers that their current products are no longer sufficient.

It appears that this is done, not through sleight of hand, but by showing you what you can't do with your current device.

By illustrating this in a manner that is contradictory to your current satisfaction, it does make you feel like your ipod – which was fine until a moment ago – has suddenly become inadequate. To me, that's really good marketing.

So what can be learned from the tens of millions that Apple spends on advertising every year? I think the answer to that question is to work in lock step with your product development team to showcase developments and tap the emotions of those using your products. When I use my iTouch, I feel empowered, cool, and complete. I wouldn't have reached that conclusion without the help of marketing to get me there.

The lesson that I've learned is that marketing, if done correctly, helps us to define how we feel about a product. Once you have prospects and customers attaching emotions to your products, you develop loyal customers. The next time that you're thinking about a marketing campaign, consider how you want your customers to feel about your product.

Manage the entire purchase decision process in order to consistently manage the experience to reinforce or produce these desired feelings. Once you've been able to do that successfully, your creative, marketing messages and promotions should be relatively easy to produce. Now that's what I call good marketing.

Notes to the text

• In the article we find the verb to feel. The basic meaning of the verb is to perceive something by touching or just having a sense, having an emotional conviction. In I feel like there is a scarcity of good marketing today the meaning is that you are convinced there is not good marketing today though you haven't got any clear evidence for it. It can also be a synonym of to think (in the article how we feel about a product means what we think about a product). When it is followed by like (feel like) it often means that someone is inclined for something or doing something.

• AmE and BrE have spelling differences: behavior/behaviour (see section at the beginning of the book) but also lexical ones. For example the word vacation is more typically American whereas the British use holiday. In AmE holiday is mainly used for religious days and imply one or more days off from school or work. Common examples of differences in the two varieties are fall (autumn BrE), cookie (biscuit BrE), zucchini (courgette BrE), faucet (tap BrE), sedan car (saloon car BrE). Some American words are also used in Britain but rarely the opposite.

• Sometimes students mix up the adjectives last and latest. For ex. the last news would refer to the order in a list, whereas the latest news would be used for the most recent news, the most updated.

Post-reading activity A 1 (Comprehension)

Answer the following questions about the article:

1. What is the author's idea of good marketing?

2. Is the ipod success due to good marketing strategies or to the product itself?

3. How can marketers convince customers that current products are no longer sufficient?

4. What do the millions of dollars spent by Apple on advertising show'

5. How can a company develop loyal customers?

6. Does good marketing have to do with reinforcing and arousing the desired feelings for the product?

Reading activity B (Comprehension/Speaking)

UK olive oil consumption on the increase

Olive oil consumption in the UK has been rising steadily over the last 19 years, according to the Office of National Statistics.

The UK share of the world consumption of olive oil has risen from 1.9% to 2.9% between 1990 and 2009. The UK now consumes 28m litres of olive oil per annum, all of which is imported, and sales topped £150m a year for the first time in 2008. This is double the amount sold eight years ago and significantly more than the £90m spent on vegetable oil. Half of UK homes now use olive oil compared with just 35% in 2001.

In recognition of this, one quarter of the total budget for the biggest promotional campaign for olive oil undertaken to date in the European Union, will be spent in the UK. ...

Launching a product in a foreign market can be one of the most profitable and rewarding activities that any entrepreneur can do. But it can also be very difficult and stressful as well. You make a very high quality extra virgin olive oil in Italy called Tuscania and you want to market it in Britain because data show that this product is increasingly valued there. By following the seven steps below work in groups and prepare a good launch of the product. Discuss ideas with your classmates:

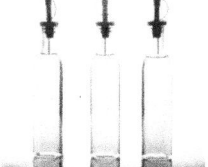

- Study your competitors
- Target your ideal customer
- Create your unique value offer
- Decide your marketing strategy
- Test product and marketing
- Present your campaign

Post-reading activity B 1 (Writing)

Choose the proverb that would best fit the article about British olive oil:

"Business opportunities are like buses, there's always another one coming." – Richard Branson, British industrialist

"Action is the foundational key to all success." – Pablo Picasso, Spanish painter

Grammar revision

-ING FORM

The –ing form can be used like a noun, an adjective or a verb:

Feeding the animals is forbidden

Fortunately, I have a short working day

If you're accustomed to working alone this may be difficult

When used like a noun it may or may not be preceded by an article:

Marketing is a waste of time

The marketing of the product was a waste of time

In formal English, we may use a possessive with the –ing form. In informal English, many speakers do not:

Despite wanting to stay local, they will go global

Despite their wanting to stay local, they will go global

When used as an adjective, the –ing form can precede a noun:

We have been granted a brief rest after the preceding months of such an intense work

The –ing form is needed after a preposition:

Despite wanting to stay local, they will go global

If you're accustomed to working alone this may be difficult

It's a time for nurturing connections with customers

Your efforts will also have a greater chance of being noticed

Many verbs are normally followed by -ing forms. Here is a list of the most common ones:

Admit (to) – appreciate – avoid – be accustomed to – be used to – can't help – consider – delay – discuss – dislike – enjoy – finish – imagine – mind – miss – postpone – recommend – regret – resist – risk – stop – suggest – understand

Other verbs can be followed by either the infinitive or –ing form but the meaning may vary. Here is a list of the most common ones:

Attempt – begin – continue – hate – like – love – neglect – prefer – remember – start – try -

For example, remember is followed by –ing form when it refers to a past event and by the infinitive when it refers to an action which is still to come:

1. I remember meeting John at a job interview.

2. I must remember to call John before 8.

In sentence 1 the action of 'meeting' precedes the action of 'remembering', whereas in sentence 2 the action of 'remembering' precedes the action of 'calling'.

Grammar exercises

1. Fill in the gaps with the right form of the verb:

a) I can't afford _____(miss) this deadline. My boss has great expectations for it.

b) If you happen _____(meet) Mr Sheen this week, please give me a ring!

c) They don't mind (help)_____ us with the backlog of work.

d) Lisa enjoys (arrive)_____ at work early in the morning.

e) We could have lunch when you finish (print)_____ those documents.

f) We shouldn't forget (call)_____ him when we leave for Berlin.

g) I would avoid (leave) _____my office unless absolutely necessary.

h) You can't stand (sell)_____! Let's be honest! If you loved it you would be more successful in your job

i) Do you appreciate (be told) _____that you deserve a promotion?

j) Paul and Sally decided (spend)_____ their lunch break in the office.

k) She regrets (not go) _____to the university two years ago when she had the chance.

l) You should remember (buy) _____some stamps in the afternoon. We have to send some letters.

m) About one in five consumers considered (move)_____ their checking accounts to another bank.

2. Fill in the gaps with the right form of the verb:

a) After (work) _____ so hard, we decided have a snack.

b) What about (have) _____ a break? It's 4 pm and I feel a little hungry.

c) Thanks for (call)_____. I really needed some friendly advice.

d) A nutcracker is essential for (remove) _____ nuts from the shell.

e) I'm looking forward to (hear) _____ from them!

f) Why can't you have a coffee without (smoke)_____? I don't like sitting alone at the bar!

g) I feel completely relaxed after (sleep) _____ 9 hours!

h) I am interested in (start) _____ a career in software engineering

i) He succeeded in (run)_____ a new business! Would you have expected this?

3. Each of the word below is written in BrE. Give the American equivalent:

Behaviour _____

Labour   _____

Metre   _____

Centre   _____

Organise   _____

Catalogue _____

Anaesthesia _____

Enrol   _____

Sizeable   _____

Chapter 5
INTERCULTURAL COMMUNICATION NEGOTIATION

Pre-reading activity

Before reading the article below try to answer the following question:

What is culture?

_____

_____

Let's see three definitions of culture given by anthropologists and sociologists. They regard culture as:

...everything that people have, think and do as members of their society (Gary P. Ferraro, 2006)

...a system of inherited conceptions expressed in symbolic forms by means of which people communicate, perpetuate, and develop their knowledge about and attitudes towards life (Clifford Geertz, 1973)

...the collective programming of the mind which distinguishes the members of one group or category of people from another (Geert Hofstede, 1997)

Culture seems to be the element characterising societies, groups and communities for their specific values, behaviours and beliefs and as such is different from country to country. Can you explain with your own words the definitions above? Which one seems to be the most suitable description of what culture is?

What is intercultural communication?
_____
_____

Intercultural communication is

...the interpersonal interaction between members of different groups, which differ from each other in respect of the knowledge shared by their members and in respect of their linguistic forms of symbolic behaviour (Karlfried Knapp, 1978)

Reading activity

Read the article below:

Intercultural Communication

An Internet search on the topic of intercultural communication or cross-cultural communication yields over 100 000 results. In recent years practitioners in a wide variety of fields—scientific cooperation, academic research, business, management, education, health, culture, politics, diplomacy, development, and others—have realised just how important intercultural communication is for their everyday work. Fast travel, international media, and the Internet have made it easy for us to communicate with people all over the world. The process of economic globalisation means that we cannot function in isolation but must interact with the rest of the world for survival. The global nature of many widely diverse modern problems and issues such as the environment, governance of the Internet, poverty and international terrorism call for cooperation between nations. Intercultural communication is no longer an option, but a necessity.

Because important decisions in business, politics, education, health, and culture these days usually effect citizens of more than one nation, the question of whether communication between people of different nations is effective and whether all parties emerge with the same understanding is of crucial importance. Individuals who deal with people from other cultures want to learn how to improve their performance through improving their communication skills. Numerous resources have sprung up to meet this emerging market in the business, academic and international relations communities: leading authors have written books and articles on the topic; business services provide consultation for improving the conduct of international business; universities and other educational institutions offer programs or degrees in Intercultural Communication; and researchers have established international journals and academic societies specialising in research on intercultural communication. In fact, intercultural communication has become a business in itself.

...

Why is it important to improve intercultural communication?

Lack of knowledge of another culture can lead, at the best, to embarrassing or amusing mistakes in communication. At the worst, such mistakes may confuse or even offend the people we wish to communicate with, making the conclusion of business deals or international agreements difficult or impossible.

Notes to the text

• By general rule the plural of nouns is formed by adding an –s to nouns ending in consonant such as bond/bonds and –es for those ending in ch/sh/x/s/o: box/boxes, witch/witches, bus/buses, hero/heroes. There are some exceptions to the rule. For ex. many nouns of foreign origin just add –s to the singular form: canto/cantos, piano/pianos, kimono/kimonos. Some words ending in y- require –es and others only -s. If y is preceded by a consonant we have y>ies as in society/societies, otherwise just –s: boy/boys. Some words ending in –f, -fe change to v+es like thief/thieves, knife/knives.

• Irregular plurals may be divided as follows: nouns with no plural form: aircraft, bison, buffalo, fish, salmon, trout, etc. –en plurals: ox/oxen, child/children, etc. – mutated plurals: foot/feet, goose/geese, tooth/teeth, man/men, mouse/mice, etc. –miscellaneous plurals: person/people, penny/pence, etc.

• Another group of irregular plural nouns are those derived from Latin and Greek such as criterion/criteria, formula/formulae (formulas), index/indices, crisis/crises, analysis/analyses, medium/media, alumnus/alumni, phenomenon/phenomena, etc.

Post-reading activity 1 (Speaking)

Interpersonal communication is the process of conveying information from at least one person to another. The information/message is sent by a sender to a receiver by means of verbal elements (words), non-verbal elements (gesture and body language) and paralanguage (voice tonality). Paralanguage can be considered a part on non-verbal language as it consists of sound levels, tone variations, inflections and pauses.

Some research indicates that communication is mainly based on non-verbal elements rather than on language:

- 55% of the message is conveyed by body language
- 38% by the tone of voice
- 7% by the words used

Read the non-verbal elements below and say what they suggest to you (openness, closeness, intimacy, shyness, etc.). Discuss with your mates:

You stand 1 metre away from someone (Proxemics)

You communicate face-to-face (Orientation)

You sit side by side (Orientation)

You keep your legs crossed (Posture)

Your arms are folded (Posture)

You slouch (Posture)

You stand up straight (Posture)

You shaking hands (Gesture)

You embrace someone (Gesture)

You give someone a pat on the back (Gesture)

You point at someone (Gesture)

You smile at someone (Facial expression)

You frown at someone (Facial expression)

You yawn when someone is speaking (Facial expression)

You sneer at someone (Facial expression)

You stare at someone (Eye contact)

After discussing the above aspects of non-verbal communication think of the differences they may have in other cultures. For example, if you show your thumb held upwards it means "everything is ok" in most American and European countries, while it is rude and offensive in some Islamic and Asian countries.

Post-reading activity 2 (Writing)

Choose the proverb/quote that would best fit the article about intercultural communication:

"I imagine hell like this: Italian punctuality, German humour and English wine." - Peter Ustinov

"All lasting business is built on friendship." – Alfred A. Montapert, American author

Post-reading activity 3 (Language and culture)

Politeness behaviours

Visitors to Britain, especially people who do business there, often complain that the British are somewhat fanatical about politeness and good manners. Their communication is filled with politeness markers and behavioural rules that cannot be neglected. In the UK if you avoid saying 'please' or 'thank you' or if you use the wrong word order in a sentence it can be considered rude and disrespectful. Also answering a question too directly can make people think you are impolite and bad-mannered.

"I agree with you entirely" or "Well, you had some good points, but you may want to consider…"

The sentences above are an example of what linguists call mitigated linguistic constructions. They are very important to mediate hostility and to establish cooperation and empathy. International negotiators know this very well and they use them effectively in business negotiations.

Agreeing with an opinion

We use these words and phrases to agree with someone else's point of view:

- Of course.
- You're absolutely right.
- Yes, I agree.
- I think so too.
- That's a good point.
- Exactly.
- I don't think so either.
- So do I
- That's true.
- Neither do I.
- I agree with you entirely.

- That's just what I was thinking.
- I couldn't agree more

Disagreeing politely with an opinion

We use these words and phrases to disagree with someone else's point of view:

- However...
- That's not entirely true.
- I take your point, but that's not the way I see it.
- I see what you mean but I'm not at all convinced that...
- I'm sorry to disagree with you, but...
- Yes, but don't you think that...
- There may be some truth in what you say but don't you think
- I'm afraid I have to disagree.
- I'm not so sure about that.

Best avoided (Don't use the following forms to express disagreement)

- I don't think so.
- No way.
- I totally disagree.
- I'd say the exact opposite.
- Not necessarily.
- That's not true.

Post-reading activity 4 (Speaking)

Intercultural misunderstanding is a very easy trap to fall into, in both language and behaviour. Read the following examples and comment on them:

A Japanese manager in an American company was told to give critical feedback to a subordinate during a performance evaluation. Japanese use high context language and are uncomfortable giving direct and confrontive feedback. It took the manager five tries before he could be direct enough to discuss the poor performance so that the American understood.

... when a Briton says "I hear what you say", the foreign listener may understand: "He accepts my point of view." In fact, the British speaker means: "I disagree and I do not wish to discuss it any further."

General Motors couldn't understand why the Chevy Nova was not selling well in Latin America, until they were told that in Spanish, "no va" means "it doesn't go".

Post-reading activity 5 (Writing)

HOW SHOULD I STRUCTURE MY ESSAY?

Most essays consist of three parts: the introduction, the body and the conclusion. If you follow this structure the content of your essay will be easily written and organised.

The beginning of the essay is the first paragraph, which is called the introduction. It consists of few sentences (three or four) that set up the topic of discussion. First you will explain what the essay will be about by trying to draw the readers' attention. Then, you will include a short summary of what readers should expect to see. After that, you will summarise what your essay will tell them and what they will learn by reading it.

The second part of the essay is called the body. It is made up of at least three paragraphs with three to five sentences. Each of the paragraphs should contain a sort of numbered sequence for the reader to follow. So, in your first paragraph you should use expressions such as first, beginning, to begin with, the first, firstly and so on. Obviously, the second paragraph will contain the next number in sequence such as secondly, next, second and so on.

Of course you must support what you wrote in the introductory paragraph and the information provided in the introduction will be developed and justified. In the last paragraph of the body you should support the last reason you provided in the introduction so that you could help the reader to reach the same conclusion as in the final part of the essay. Always support the facts with examples and, to finish provide a conclusion based on the facts and examples.

We are now moving on to the final paragraph of the essay: the conclusion. This part consists of three or four sentences and sums up the whole essay. You will use expressions such as in conclusion, in summary, finally, lastly and so on to point out that the essay is going to finish. In the last sentence you will state your conclusion and include thus, I conclude, therefore, based on the above facts it can be concluded, I will, you will, they will and so on.

Of course there may be different types of essays. There are "agree/disagree" essays where you are supposed to give your opinion related to a given statement or a "pros and cons" essay in which you should list advantages and disadvantages of something and justify them. In addition there are expository essays where you are supposed to give explanation about an issue or an idea to an audience. Analytical essays, which examine an event, a book or a poem. There are other types of essays and each of them is connected with a different purpose.

Let us look together this essay model based on an IELTS writing test. After reading the title and the model essay, work on the chart given below and fill in the empty column on the right in order to determine whether the essay given conforms to the general rules for a good essay:

"Some of the methods used in advertising are unethical and unacceptable in today's society. To what extent do you agree with this view?"

The world that we live in today is dominated by advertising. Adverts are on television, on the World Wide Web, in the street and even on our mobile phones. However, many of the strategies used to sell a product or service can be considered immoral or unacceptable.

To begin with, the fact that we cannot escape from advertising is a significant cause for complaint. Constant images and signs wherever we look can be very intrusive and irritating at times. Take for example advertising on the mobile phone. With the latest technology mobile companies are now able to send advertising messages via SMS to consumer's phones whenever they choose. Although we expect adverts in numerous situations, it now seems that there are very few places we can actually avoid them.

A further aspect of advertising that I would consider unethical is the way that it encourages people to buy products they may not need or cannot afford. Children and young people in particular are influenced by adverts showing the latest toys, clothing or music and this can put enormous pressure on the parents to buy these products.

INTRODUCTION	First you will explain what the essay will be about by trying to draw the reader's attention.	*The world that we live in today is dominated by advertising.*
	Then, you will include a short summary of what readers should expect to see.	
	After that, you will summarize what your essay will tell them and what he will learn by reading it.	
BODY	So, in your first paragraph you should use expressions such as *first, to begin with, the first, firstly* and so on.	
	The second paragraph will contain the next number in sequence such as *secondly, next, second* and so on. Of course you must support what you wrote in the introductory paragraph and the information provided in the	

	introduction will be developed and justified.
	In the last paragraph of the *body* you should support the last reason you provided in the introduction so that you could help the reader to reach the same conclusion as in the final part of the essay. Always support the facts with examples and, to finish provide a conclusion based on the facts and examples
CONCLUSION	This part consists of three or four sentences and sums up the whole essay. You will use expressions such as *in conclusion, in summary, finally, lastly* and so on to point out that the essay is going to finish. In the last sentence you will state your conclusion and include *thus, I conclude, therefore, based on the above facts it can be concluded, I will, you will* and so on.

In addition, the advertising of tobacco products and alcohol has long been a controversial issue, but cigarette adverts have only recently been banned in many countries. It is quite possible that alcohol adverts encourage excessive consumption and underage drinking, yet restrictions have not been placed on this type of advertising in the same way as smoking.

It is certainly true to say that advertising is an everyday feature of our lives. Therefore, people are constantly being encouraged to buy products or services that might be too expensive, unnecessary or even unhealthy. In conclusion, many aspects of advertising do appear to be morally wrong and are not acceptable in today's society. (296 words)

Post-reading activity 6 (Writing)

Essay writing:

During the last decades technology has changed our lives in many ways, and more people are using it in their daily life. The Internet, the mobile phone, home banking and other technological devices have become a part of everybody's life. In most cases they have made our lives easier but some people may get addicted to it. Discuss the pros and cons of technology and give reasons for your opinion.

Grammar revision

PASSIVE FORM

ACTIVE SENTENCE: Advertising dominates the world we live in

PASSIVE SENTENCE: The world we live in is dominated by advertising

In the active form the object receives the action of the subject. This is the most used type of sentence in the language. In the passive form the object of the active verb becomes the subject of the sentence.

The passive form is normally used when it is not necessary or deliberately decided to say who did the action or the doer is unknown:

Cigarette adverts have only recently been banned

In this sentence we do not know or we think it is unimportant to say who has banned cigarette adverts . Or simply it is taken for granted, it is obvious that we are referring to a specific context which is familiar to the interlocutor (the government, regulators).

Of course we could also say:

Cigarette adverts have only recently been banned (by our government)

By is used in the passive voice to introduce the agent:

Our government has only recently banned cigarette adverts

Subject + to be + past participle

To be + subject + past participle   (+ by...)

Subject + to be + past particple

Restrictions have not been placed on this type of advertising

People are constantly being encouraged to buy products or services...

Many of the strategies used to sell a product or service can be considered immoral or unacceptable

Grammar exercises

1. Fill in the gaps with the right passive form of the verb given in brackets:

1. The brand needs (improve)_____ and (consolidate)_____

2. A lot of money will (spend)_____ marketing campaigns as well

3. The game of telephone won't (play)_____ in our company.

4. The rules need (to spell out)_____.

5. Agree on a follow-up date to check which next steps have (take)_____.

6. The 10-month union was (hurt)_____ by regular cultural clashes.

7. The idea came after my old start-up was (sell off)_____.

8. The name of the company might even (change)_____.

9. In March the first store will (open)_____.

10. We haven't (intimidate)_____ by veteran entrepreneurs.

2. Fill in the gaps with the right passive form of the verb given in brackets:

Our business plan (1. Suggest) _____ in late 2009 by our consultants during regular meetings. It (2. Develop)_____ in January-May 2009 in a consultative process involving all stakeholders and (3. Approve)_____ by the Executive Board at its second meeting in June 2009. Then, it (4. Update)_____ in July 2010 and (5. review) will _____ further _____ at future Board meetings.

Oranges (1. Grow)_____ in warm climates throughout the world. The taste of oranges may vary from sweet to sour. The fruit (2. Peel)_____ generally _____and (3. Eat)_____ fresh, or (4. Squeeze)_____ for its juice. The skin of an orange is thick and bitter so it (5. Discard)_____ usually _____, but it can (6. Process)_____ into animal feed by removing water using pressure and heat.

Chapter 6
PEOPLE MONEY

Pre-reading activity 1

Before reading the article below, answer the following questions:

What does money mean to you?

Does money make the world go around?

What does the expression "Money doesn't grow on trees" mean?

Can money buy happiness?

Do you think this saying is true? "Money is the root of all evil"

People with a lot of money are often called rich, but there are a lot of other ways to mean the same thing, though with slight differences:

billionaire

A billionaire is someone who possesses assets worth at least a billion pounds or dollars. The word is derived from billion and follows the pattern of millionaire.

Similar words

- man of wealth
- man of means
- capitalist
- tycoon
- magnate
- rich man
- moneyed man
- plutocrat
- Nabob /ˈneɪbɒb/
- Midas /ˈmʌɪdəs/
- man of millions
- financier
- fat cat
- big cheese

- wealthy man
- parvenu
- nouveau riche
- Croesus /ˈkriːsəs/

Some of the words on the list may have a derogatory sense, others are informal. Can you find them? Do some of the expressions also exist in your language? If you need help work with a dictionary

Pre-reading activity 2 (Speaking)

Read the information below about Forbes, a very well-known American magazine. Then, answer the questions and move on to pre-reading activity 2:

Forbes is an American business magazine owned by Forbes, Inc. It is published every two weeks and it shows articles on finance, business, investing, and marketing topics. It also deals with related themes such as technology, communications, lifestyles and so on. Headquarters are in New York City. Its major competitors as national business magazines are Fortune and Bloomberg Businessweek. The magazine is famous for its lists, such as those related to the

1) richest Americans (the Forbes 400)

2) highest-paid stars under 30

3) list of billionaires.

The motto of Forbes magazine is "The Capitalist Tool".

Questions:

1. What is Forbes?
2. What is the magazine about?
3. Where is it headquartered?
4. Who are its main competitors?
5. Why is the magazine so well-known?
6. What does Forbes' motto mean?

Pre-reading activity 3 (Writing/Speaking)

Look up the number of billionaires in the world (2013) available at Wikipedia.org. It provides the names of countries with the highest number of billionaires and some related data. This kind of list is drawn up annually by the Forbes Magazine and it leaves out heads of states whose prosperity is tied to their position.

Figures are given for the number of billionaires in specific countries, with share of world total, the number of billionaires per ten million people and the category (here, you are supposed to fill in the right nationality adjective):

World wide top 10 (2013)

Rank	Country/Region	Number of billionaires	Share of world total (%)	Billionaires per 10M	Category
—	World total		100.0		
1					_____ billionaires
2					_____ billionaires
3					_____ billionaires
4					_____ billionaires
5					_____ billionaires
6					_____ billionaires
7					_____ billionaires
8					_____ billionaires
9					_____ billionaires
10					_____ billionaires

Questions:

Are you surprised at the results?

Did you expect to find other countries on the list?

Do you think the share of the world total will soon increase in some of the countries on the list?

Are the BRIC countries on the list?

Italy is not on the list. Give your reasons for it.

Reading activity

The article below is divided into two parts. First read part 1 and answer the questions. Then do the same with part 2. After that read the whole article again, note down the main information and try to summarise the whole article:

Italian Fitness Founder

How an Exercise Machine Turned into an International Wellness Empire

Part 1

Nerio Alessandri was only 22 years old when he designed his first exercise machine in his parents' garage. Soon, a local gym in his hometown of Cesena, Italy, bought some of his equipment, and a larger gym in the area commissioned 30 machines. "I took the order even though I had no team and no company premises apart from my parents' garage," Alessandri says. "This was the time I decided to dedicate myself full time to the Technogym project and to start up a proper company."

That was 1983, and today, Technogym has 13 international branches, equipping more than 35,000 wellness centers and 20,000 private homes all over the world. The company furnishes machines for European soccer teams, Ferrari Formula One drivers and was the official supplier for multiple

Olympic Games, including the 2008 Games in Beijing. Alessandri has won several international design awards, and he was the Ernst & Young Italian Entrepreneur of the Year in 2003. Oh, and he's a knight. In fact, he's the youngest person to receive the Cavaliere del Lavoro (Italian industry knighthood) in history.

All of this is the result of his pioneering attitude toward fitness. During the aerobics-crazy '80s and '90s, Alessandri took a different approach, creating a culture of wellness that expanded the notion of health to include diet and a positive mental approach. Alessandri calls it "psycho-physical wellness."

Today, he encourages other business owners to think of wellness as an investment in more productive and motivated staff: "At Technogym, we strongly believe that employees' health and happiness represent both a corporate social responsibility and an economic asset for the company. That's why we provide a comprehensive corporate wellness scheme for our staff including a complete gym and a personalized wellness program for each employee with a training program and medical and nutritional counseling." And Alessandri walks his talk. "I never miss my three times per week early morning workout," he says. Although he does admit to indulging in a huge meal with family and friends now and then, as well as enjoying "a few glasses of red wine from my own vineyards." Now that's good living.

Post-reading activity 1 (Comprehension)

Answer the following questions:

1. Where did Nerio Alessandri use to work and design his machines at the beginning of his career?
2. Who are Technogyn's major customers?
3. When was he awarded the Ernst & Young prize? Why?
4. What is meant by "psycho-physical wellness"?
5. How does he regard staff's wellness?
6. How often does he work out per week?

Big Business in a Small Town

How Cesena, Italy, Became the Heart of the Wellness Valley

Part 2

Despite rapid growth and an international supply chain, Nerio Alessandri's fitness company Technogym is still headquartered in his small hometown of Cesena, Italy. Why not move the base of operations to a larger, more metropolitan location?

"I have very strong ties with my region," Alessandri says, "and I strongly believe that Technogym and the wellness lifestyle were not born there by chance. Romagna, our region, is well-known in Italy and in Europe for its balance between quality of life, economic wealth, good public services and people's hospitality."

In 2003, Alessandri launched the Wellness Foundation, a nonprofit that focuses on research, health education and cultural initiatives, with a special emphasis on the local area. The "Wellness Valley, Romagna Benessere" project aims to establish the region as a leader in quality of life.

"Many local stakeholders followed us in this initiative by creating a lot of wellness-based best practices," Alessandri says. Businesses, government institutions, universities and the tourism industry have joined him in his quest to create an oasis in the fertile Italian valley where his company was born. Wellness holidays on the coast, health courses at universities, free checkups for citizens and citywide walking initiatives are just a few of the ways Alessandri's concept of whole-life health has spread through the region.

So it makes sense to keep his company in Cesena, a place that has eagerly adopted the company's concept of wellness. Last year, Romagna was ranked first in a happiness survey by Il Sole 24 Ore, an Italian financial newspaper.

Answer the following questions:

1. Why is Technogym still headquartered in Cesena?

2. What is the Wellness Foundation?

3. How has Alessandri spread the concept of whole-life spread?

4. So, does it still make sense to keep the company in Cesena?

Post-reading activity 2 (Writing)

Based on what you have read, try to complete the chart below. It is about Alessandri's main events, activities and business ideas throughout his life:

He was _____ in 19__ in Cesena.	?n he was 22 he _____ _____ _____	Soon a local gym_____ and a larger gym _____
So 1983 was the year when he decided _____ _____ _____	ay Technogym h_____. It ps	Its main clients are _____ _____ _____ _____
_____ _____ _____	..._ _____	...ok another approach to fitness and _____ _____

ay he thinks that loyees' health ar ___ ___	He works out three ___ ___ ___	He drinks red ___ ___ ___
says he hasn't iged Technogym lquarters becaus ___ ___	The Wellness Foundation was ___ in 2003. It is a ___ ___	Alessandri's concept of whole-life health is based on ___ ___ ___

Grammar revision

LINKING WORDS

They are words and short phrases which link sentences, paragraphs and sections and so are cohesive devices. They perform different functions such as giving examples, adding information, summarising, sequencing ideas, contrasting and so on.

Giving examples

For example

For instance

Namely

Adding information

And

In addition

As well as

Also

Too

Furthermore

Moreover

Apart from

In addition to

Besides

Ideas are often linked by and. Also is used to add an extra idea or to give more emphasis.

If you start a sentence you can use In addition or In addition to this...

As well as is both used at the beginning or the middle of a sentence.

Too and as well are synonyms of also.

Apart from and besides are often used to mean as well as, or in addition to.

Moreover and furthermore provide extra information to what you are saying.

Summarising

In short

In brief

In summary

To summarise

To conclude

In conclusion

We generally use these words at the start of the sentence to give a summary of what we have said or written.

Sequencing ideas

The former, ... the latter

Firstly, secondly, finally

The first point is

Lastly

The following

The former and the latter are used when you refer to one of two points.

Firstly, ... secondly, ... finally (or lastly) are used to list ideas.

The following can be used to start a list.

Giving a reason

Due to / due to the fact that

Owing to / owing to the fact that

Because

Because of

Since

As

Due to and owing to are followed by a noun or you must follow the words with the fact that.

Because / because of

Because of is followed by a noun.

Because can be used at the beginning or in the middle of a sentence.

Since / as

Since and as mean because.

Giving a result

Therefore

So

Consequently

This means that

As a result

Therefore, so, consequently, as a result are all used similarly. So is more informal.

Contrasting ideas

But

However

Although / even though

Despite / despite the fact that

In spite of / in spite of the fact that

Nevertheless

Nonetheless

While

Whereas

Unlike

In theory... in practice...

But is more informal than however.

Although, despite and in spite of bring in an idea of contrast.

Despite and in spite of are used in the same way as due to and owing to. They are followed by a noun. If you want to follow them with a noun and a verb, you must use the fact that.

Nevertheless and nonetheless mean in spite of that or anyway.

While, whereas and unlike show how two things are different from each other.

In theory... in practice... show an unexpected result.

Grammar exercises

1. Choose the correct linking word

1. In addition/in theory/because of to providing information on their firm's products, these workers help prospective and current buyers with technical problems.

2. Almost 50 percent of home foreclosures are owing to/due to/due to the fact that unemployment or loss of income.

3. Owing to the fact/owing to/because of that the weather was cold, we stayed home.

4. Tom and Dick were both heroes but only the firstly/the former/the following is remembered today.

5. As described in section 2, the former are the originally reported unemployment rate as well as/also/too the turnover rate.

6. Taking parental leave does not affect other employment rights you have. In addition/Since/Apart from the loss of pay and pension contributions, your position remains as if no parental leave had been taken

7. The company undertakes to respect privacy of the information given and not to resell such information to third parties. Nevertheless/In spite of/Despite, the company cannot guarantee secrecy of correspondences on the internet network,

8. In short/unlike/since, the CEO agreed to settle Company B's debt by issuing new, unregistered shares of stock worth as much as five times, or more, than the debt that Company B actually owed.

9. The first point is/because of/lastly, the Firm advises all customers that as the cause, effect and length of a significant business disruption cannot be determined with certainty, the customer should plan in advance his/her actions.

10. As a result/even though/whereas, politicians like any other individual or corporation, are very concerned about their brand.

Chapter 7
PEOPLE STRATEGIES

Pre-reading activity

Before reading the article below, answer the following question:

What is strategy?

_____

_____

According to the Oxford English Dictionary the word strategy refers to a plan of action designed to achieve a long-term or overall aim.

In business we talk about strategic management. Wikipedia defines it as the major initiatives taken by a company's top management on behalf of owners, involving resources and performance in external environments. It entails specifying the organisation's mission, vision and objectives, developing policies and plans, often in terms of projects and programs, which are designed to achieve these objectives, and then allocating resources to implement the policies and plans, projects and programs.

What is the company's mission?

_____

What is the vision?

_____

Now you should have a more precise idea of what strategy is and what is for, so after having a look at the glossary below, move on to the reading activity:

GLOSSARY

English word/phrase	English equivalent or definition
Knack	Talent, ability
Setbacks	Difficulty, trouble, hitch
To pour into	To tip into, *fig.* to invest
Sales lead	Potential customer
Referrals	Recommendation from another individual
Exemption	Privilege, dispensation, concession
Operations and billing	Operations refers to all the activities in a business, from production to logistics, etc. Billing is the account dept.
Petty theft	Stealing property whose value is low
Pot	*Sl.* Marijuana
Stunning	Shocking
Slick	Slippery

Reading activity

Norm Brodsky's 5 Most Controversial Business Ideas

Veteran entrepreneur Norm Brodsky has made many mistakes—but he has a knack for learning from setbacks and using the knowledge gained through adversity to improve his business. Here are 5 controversial and easy-to-argue business ideas that he has come to believe in, through trial and error. You may disagree with Brodsky. That's fine with him. He is confident you will one day change your mind.

Competition is Great

When rival start-ups began to **pour into** the records-storage business, Brodsky was thrilled. "In a young industry like ours, you have to spend an inordinate amount of time and money just explaining what you do and why prospective customers should pay you to do it," he explains. The more competitors you have, the easier that task becomes." Competition makes comparison-shopping possible, which simplifies your sales pitch. All you have to do is explain to a **sales lead** why you're better than the next guy.

Employee Referrals Cause Trouble

After a series of troubles tied to employees who had recommended their friends and family for jobs, Brodsky banned the practice of hiring relatives and associates. He even fired a woman who had sought an **exemption** for her friend and, when it was not granted, hired her anyway hoping that their relationship would not be discovered. "Understand, the rule was not a matter of convenience," Brodsky says. "On the contrary, it was easier and cheaper to rely on staff recommendations… But I couldn't accept the number of good employees we were losing by hiring friends and relatives who didn't work out."

Sales Commissions Don't Work

"Commissions are the norm in most industries, and commissions are the only way to motivate some salespeople," Brodsky concedes. "But those aren't the people I want in my company, and you should think twice about having them in yours." Most salespeople want to be part of a successful team, Brodsky explains. But when you pay them by commission, you treat them differently than every other employee—and give them the means to maximize their pay even if it comes at the expense of other departments such as **operations and billing**. Instead of base plus commission, Brodsky recommends you pay a salary plus a three-part bonus tied to the success of the individual, the team, and the company.

Drug Testing is a Good Idea

Warehouse accidents, **petty theft**, and absenteeism were on the rise at Brodsky's company, and he had heard rumors that employees were smoking **pot** on the premises. So he reluctantly implemented drug testing—and the results were **stunning**. More than half of all current employees tested positive, and more than 75 percent of potential new hires tested positive. One executive secretary candidate reluctantly declined a job offer, only to reveal that she routinely smoked crack on her lunch break. After instituting random screening, the accident rate declined, as did the incidence of petty theft. Morale improved among the other workers. Another bonus: "Our drug-testing program made us more attractive to insurers, allowing us to move our policies to a better provider," Brodsky says.

Marketing is a Waste of Money

"Much of what passes for marketing these days is a waste of time and money that has nothing to do with building a good solid business," Brodsky says. A **slick** brochure or presentation lacks soul in Brodsky's view, and indicates to your customers that you are just like everyone else. Brodsky would rather have homemade marketing materials (see above) that reinforce that his business is like a family, and will treat you well. Your marketing collateral should "reflect who we are, not some marketer's idea of who we should be," he says.

The Less You're Around, the Better for the Business

Brodsky decided years ago that he wanted to take as much as 16 weeks of vacation a year. That meant that he had to train his employees to be autonomous and to not rely on him to get things done. So he started to prepare his company. His managers took on new responsibilities; customers got used to less face time with the owner; and outside investors saw Brodsky's ability to step back from the business as a plus. Best of all, the entrepreneur says he was able to ponder the business's problems with greater perspective. "It was obvious to me that I was a bigger asset to the company on my return than I had been when I left," Brodsky says.

Notes to the text

- A commission is a form of remuneration for services or products sold by an agent or a sales representative. So, some sales reps are paid on commission only, others work on a salary plus commission basis, that means they are paid a salary plus bonuses if they meet certain sales quotas. There are other forms of job remuneration. When talking about employees we use the words salary or wage. A salary is paid periodically based on the employment contract, whereas a wage is calculated at an hourly rate or on the quantity of work done. Professionals have another form of remuneration for their services, the fee, which is paid by clients to accountants, doctors, lawyers, etc.

- In the article we find the expression competition is great. The adjective grande (it.) can be translated in English with great, big or large in accordance with the context. In few words we could say that big and large are used with concrete nouns and great with abstract nouns: a big/large office and a great opportunity. Abstract nouns can precede big if they are countable: a big opportunity.

- When something is on the rise it is growing or increasing. Look at Unit 10 for trends.

- Morale and moral are respectively a noun and an adjective. The former means spirit of optimism, confidence. The latter may be an adjective meaning ethical, adhering to conventional standards of behaviour. As a noun, moral refers to a truth or a maxim often contained in fables and anecdotes.

- In the text we find some verb + particle combinations such as step back/take on/work out. They are usually called phrasal verbs and consist of the combination of a verb plus an adverb or preposition. Most phrasal verbs are idiomatic, that is the meaning of the combination is not deductible from the two elements taken separately. In some cases they may preserve a literal meaning, as a result of the locative particle which is part of the compound, like in go out/come in/bring up, but often they give rise to a completely new meaning. Some of them are polysemous, that is they can have more than one meaning:

Step back = retreat, move backwards

Take on = assume, accept; oppose, fight; employ

Work out = exercise; find a solution to; calculate or solve something; understand

Here is a list of common phrasal verbs:

apply for

make a formal request (a job)

blow up

explode

call off

cancel

fill in

write information in blanks

give up

stop trying or quit a habit

grow up

become more like an adult

hand out

give something out like papers

leave out

not include

put off

postpone an event

show up

make an appearance in a place

take off

fly away from the ground or remove clothes

turn down

decline or refuse

Post-reading activity 1 (Comprehension)

Answer the following questions about the article:

1. Why was Brodsky excited when rival start-ups began to pour into the records-storage business?

2. Why does Brodsky regard competition as a positive element?

3. Why did he decide to ban the practice of hiring employees' relatives and friends?

4. Why does he think that paying salespeople on a commission basis is not good?

5. Why did he implement drug testing in the company?

6. Why is traditional marketing regarded as a waste of money?

7. How was Brodsky able to have 16 weeks of vacation a year?

Post-reading activity 2 (Writing)

Explain with your own words how Brodsky implemented his strategy in managing his company. You should focus on the measures and initiatives he took since most new start-ups poured into the records-storage market.

_____
_____
_____
_____
_____

Post-reading activity 3 (Speaking)

Some years ago Brodsky decided to delegate some responsibilities to his managers. Some managers are not willing to delegate to others because they think there is nobody else who can do as well as they do in their job. Others think they might lose their key performance. But enlightened managers and owners know that delegation has more to do with growing people than reducing your own prestige and precious cooperation. So discuss the following issue: "Delegating responsibility. Is delegation a key skill for success or a risk of losing power?

Post-reading activity 4 (Speaking)

Explain the meaning of the following statement and say whether it is a good strategy or not:

"Always forgive your enemies; nothing annoys them so much." – Oscar Wilde, British dramatist and poet

Grammar revision

PAST PERFECT SIMPLE

I HAD CLEANED

(Used for a past action which occurred before another action in the past and it shows which event happened first).

He fired a woman who had sought an exemption for a friend

He had heard rumors that employees were smoking pot on the premises

Brodsky banned the practice of hiring relatives...who had recommended friends and families

I was a bigger asset to the company on my return than I had been when I left

Subject + had + past participle

Had + subject + past participle

Subject + had + not + past participle

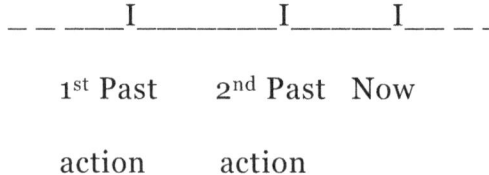

    1st Past   2nd Past Now

    action   action

PAST PERFECT CONTINUOUS

I HAD BEEN CLEANING

(Used for a past action that was in progress before another past action It is also used

with for /since to say how long that action had been in progress)

They had been talking for two hours when Paul arrived

He told me I hadn't been working hard enough that week

Had you been waiting long before the taxi arrived?

Subject + had + been + ing form

Had + subject + been + ing form

Subject + had + not + been + ing form

_ _ _IIIIIIIIIIIIIIIII _____I__ _ _

   1st Past   2nd Past   Now

action in progress   action

Post-reading activity 5 (Comprehension)

Read the article about advantages and disadvantages about delegation and see if there are new points that you did not take into consideration when discussing Activity 3:

Delegating pros and cons

Delegation, when done well by managers, produces higher productivity, higher morale, and greater workplace efficiency. However, two common situations prevent many managers from succeeding at this skill as well as they could.

First, managers usually know that the task they're delegating will likely NOT be done as well as they could do it themselves. They will probably experience an immediate decrease in productivity by delegating that task. Not good. When environments are demanding, managers may feel too much pressure to take time for proper delegating. A long view is needed to invest in employees by delegating. Counsel them too, to deserve that investment.

Another barrier is the fear of being made irrelevant by delegating tasks central to one's key performance. People tend to identify with their job tasks especially when they become proficient at them. Intentionally giving away those tasks, especially to someone who may eventually be better at it than you, can be intimidating. Managers need to courageously decide to do what is best and give up some of their power for the sake of the greater good. I have talked to many managers who longed for their old tasks, long ago delegated to others. Remember in your new role, you're expected to go on to management tasks.

Delegation is more about growing people than it is reducing your own work load. It communicates that you trust someone enough to give them higher responsibility for key results. It provides a context for coaching, accountability, and training. Learn the art and skills of wise delegation and reap the benefits of greater leadership and effectiveness

DELEGATION VERSUS EMPOWERMENT

Some people tend to mix up the words, but according to Gary Runn, an executive Director for Leadership Development, the two terms are different and should not be used interchangeably. Look up the two words in a dictionary and the read the short extract given below.

To delegate means to choose or elect a person to act as a representative for another.

To empower someone means to give power or authority to someone else. Do you hear the difference? To delegate something to someone is to only give them enough leash to act on your behalf-as you would for yourself. To empower another means you give them enough power and authority to act on their own behalf (Gary Runn)

In few words we can say that delegation and empowerment have some points in common but they differ in that:

Delegation is _____

Empowerment is _____

Supplementary activity (Listening)

Read some introductory information about Charles Tyrwhitt, the company managed by Nick Wheeler. Then go to YouTube and listen to Nick Wheeler's interview about empowerment (Empowering staff is good for business) and try to note down his main ideas on the topic.

Charles Tyrwhitt (pronounced "Tirrit") produces fine menswear. The company started to do business in 1986 aiming to make a shirt better than anybody else. In addition to formal and casual shirts, the store offers a variety of accessories, including ties, belts, evening wear, coats and shoes. Their casual collection includes polo shirts and slacks. They also make women's clothes, from shirts to knitwear and accessories.

Nick Wheeler, the CEO of Charles Tyrwhitt is convinced that giving his staff the freedom to decide can really pay off. Nick

Wheeler shows how giving his staff at Charles Tyrwhitt the freedom to make decisions can really have good consequences for both the company and customers.

Empowering staff is good for business because

_____
_____
_____
_____
_____

Grammar revision

COMPARATIVES AND SUPERLATIVES

COMPARATIVES

Adjectives have a comparative degree::

comparatives of majority are formed by adding the suffix – ER to the adjective:

OLD = OLDER

Longer adjectives are preceded by MORE:

INTELLIGENT = MORE INTELLIGENT

The second element of a comparison is introduced by THAN:

Paul is 25 years old

John is 20 years old

Paul is older than John

My jacket costs 200 euros

Your trousers cost 100 euros

My jacket is more expensive than your trousers

Some adjectives have irregular comparatives:

GOOD = BETTER

BAD = WORSE

FAR = FARTHER/FURTHER

Also adverbs and verbs can be compared:

It's more difficult to write than to phone

It's better late than never

You say ...THAN ME, YOU, HIM, HER, US, THEM

I can write faster than him

The comparative of minority is LESS... THAN

Paul is less tall than Chris

English is less difficult than Chinese

That movie was less interesting than this one

The comparative of equality is:

AS.... AS

I'm not as tall as Matthew

It isn't as hot as yesterday

AS MUCH (...) AS – AS MANY (...) AS

I don't eat as much as you

They have as many friends as me

THE SAME AS... is used to say

My car is not the same colour as yours

Grammar exercises

1. Put the following sentences in the correct form of the past perfect simple:

1. When the meeting started nobody knew some investors _____ (decide) to fund our business.

2. This attitude clashed with the pragmatic approach Corning _____ (develop) over decades of competition

3. After a series of troubles tied to employees who _____ (recommend) their friends and family for jobs, Brodsky banned the practice of hiring relatives and associates.

4. He _____ (hear) rumors that employees were smoking pot on the premises.

5. He even fired a woman who _____ (seek) an exemption for her friend

6. The LSL study also found that tenant arrears _____ (improve).

7. It took a long time to realize that the business _____ (fail) for many reasons

8. There was absolutely no training for my management position when I started 1 year ago as the manager _____ (quit) months before.

9. Reports showed bank profits _____ (grow) principally because banks were just cleaning up bad loans.

10. There was a lot of discontent when these customers eventually found that the products _____ (sell out).

2. Put the following adjective in brackets in the correct form of the comparative:

1. A car is _____ than a bicycles. (heavy)

2. My car runs _____ than yours. (fast)

3. The prince is _____ than the king. (elegant)

4. Stephen is a _____ lawyer than Jack. (good)

5. Bicycles are _____ than motorbikes. (safe)

6. August is _____ than February. (long)

7. A cat is _____ than a tiger. (dangerous)

8. Jane is _____ than Martha. (happy)

9. Smartphones are _____ than tablets. (expensive)

10. I think golf is _____ as football. (tedious)

3. Fill in the blanks with the correct phrasal verbs

1. He _____ his raincoat and sat on the sofa.

2. The plane _____ after a three hour delay.

3. Rebecca _____ the job offer because the salary was too low.

4. Because of the rain, the exhibition was _____ until Monday.

5. Listen, please! _____ question 8 – it is wrong.

6. Could you please _____ these forms.

7. I want to _____ smoking but I can't

8. I have tried to _____ which is better, but it's almost impossible!

9. They rarely attend the course. They just _____ when they want.

10. A bomb _____ while police was towing a car that was loaded with explosives

4. Replace the word/expression in bold with a suitable phrasal verb:

1. If you are really interested in that job just **write a formal application and send it**

2. The meeting **was cancelled** because the majority of the members were not present

3. If you wish to be contacted by our staff, please **write information in** this form

4. I have often tried **to stop** drinking but I have never succeeded

5. While doing exercise 5, please **don't include** the second sentence. It is wrong!

6. The concert **has been postponed** because of the heavy rain

7. She **refused** the invitation because most of the guests were unsociable and snobby

Chapter 8
PEOPLE SUCCESS

Pre-reading activity

Before reading the article about success, try to answer the following question:

What does success mean to you?
_____
_____

Now read the following statements about success and have your say:

"Success is getting what you want. Happiness is wanting what you get." B. R. Hayden

"Success is a journey, not a destination." Ben Sweetland

"Failure is success if we learn from it." Malcolm S. Forbes

"Success is the ability to go from failure to failure without losing your enthusiasm." Winston Churchill

"There's no secret about success. Did you ever know a successful man who didn't tell you about it?" Kin Hubbard

"Success usually comes to those who are too busy to be looking for it." Henry David Thoreau

Which statement best describes your idea of success? Why?

_____
_____
_____
_____

Test Your Attitude Towards Success

The quantity of success you may have in life is strongly related to the approach you have towards success. Do you know what is your attitude towards success? What does that mean for you? Take the 5-minute test below; you may be surprised at the results you get. Select one of the three answers to the questions below, and then compute your score as shown in Appendix 4 key to exercises:

TEST

1

(A) I have a clear idea of what success means to me.

(B) I have no idea what success means to me.

(C) I have somewhat of an idea what success means to me.

2

(A) I always seek advice and feedback.

(B) I never seek advice and feedback.

(C) Sometimes I seek advice and feedback.

3

(A) I never give up something I enjoy now, for something better in the future.

(B) Sometimes I give up something I enjoy now, for something better in the future

(C) I always give up something I enjoy now, for something better in the future.

4

(A) When I have a setback or rejection, I give up and quit

(B) When I have a setback or rejection,I learn from it and try again

(C) Sometime setbacks or rejection causes me to quit, other times I try again.

5

(A) I believe I will be successful.

(B) I believe I will never be successful.

(C) Maybe I will be successful, maybe I will not

6

(A) I am always fully prepared for the things I do.

(B) I am never prepared for the things I do.

(C) Sometimes I am prepared and other times I am not.

7

(A) I would never take a risk, I only want sure things.
(B) I am somewhat open to taking risks.
(C) I am willing to take risks if the rewards seem worth it

8

(A) What happens in my life is not my responsibility.

(B) What happens in my life is somewhat my responsibility.

(C) What happens in my life is totally my responsibility.

9

(A) Change always brings me new opportunities.

(B) Change never brings me new opportunities.

(C) Change sometimes brings me new opportunities.

10

(A) I go all out when I am working on something.

(B) I hold back somewhat when I am working on something.

(C) I never go all out when I am working on something.

Reading activity

Secrets to Fascinating Anyone

Sally Hogshead, author of Fascinate: Your Seven Triggers to Persuasion and Captivation explains how to exploit your own personality traits in order to surprise someone thoroughly.

Sally Hogshead is the author of a book called Fascinate: Your Seven Triggers to Persuasion and Captivation, and as such she addresses audiences who will feel deceived if they aren't enchanted by her words. The audience at the Inc. Leadership Forum in Miami seemed appropriately rapt--especially when Hogshead explained what makes them different from the rest of the world.

In her book, Hogshead says the triggers are--passion, power, trust, mystique, prestige, alarm and rebellion--that transform a brand from a utility into something people want to talk about and buy. Those triggers can do the same thing for people as for companies and products, Hogshead explained.

Trouble is, many people don't recognize their special, hardwired qualities that, when leveraged to their fullest, make them memorable. Those qualities are a leader's most unique competitive advantage. "It's why certain leaders have so many followers and certain salespeople always seal the deal," said Hogshead.

Worried you can't learn to be fascinating? All you have to do is unlearn how to be boring, Hogshead said. "Your brain is hardwired to fascinate. It's a survival mechanism," she explained.

But different people fascinate in different ways. Some take command, some use emotion, some arouse curiosity, some inspire respect, some create urgency, some build loyalty, and some change the game. Everyone does one or more of these things in every interaction every day. But they don't always use the right one or the one that best suits their personality.

Hogshead advised conference attendees on identifying the fascination triggers associated with their own personalities and how to use them in everything from hiring to introducing themselves. How important is it to recognize and exploit your fascination triggers? People pay up to four times more for a fascinating brand, says Hogshead. When the audience heard that, they were fascinated.

Post-reading activity 1 (Comprehension)

Read the statements below and say whether they are true or false:

1. Sally Hogshead thinks personality traits can be exploited in order to surprise someone thoroughly.
   T F

2. Her audiences usually feel deceived by her enchanting words T F

3. Some triggers used to transform a utility into a product are the same that can be used for people
   T F

4. People are rarely aware of their best qualities
   T F

5. Boringness is the worst enemy to people's fascination
   T F

6. People fascinate the others all in the same way
   T F

7. Hogshead's advice to her trainees is to find out what are the fascination triggers associated with their personality in order to make the most of them.
   T F

8. Hogshead says that fascinating brand have a higher value for which people are willing to pay much more

    T F

Post-reading activity 2 (Speaking)

Do you think Sally Hogshead's secrets to fascinating people are good advice? Do you think there are good strategies and techniques in order to be admired and highly-valued? Discuss

Grammar revision

PRESENT SIMPLE

I CLEAN (Habitual action, repeated action, scientific truth)

In her book Hogshead says that triggers transform a brand

Many people don't recognize their special qualities

But different people fascinate in different ways

Some use emotion, some arouse curiosity, some inspire respect

I always seek advice and feedback.

Change always brings me new opportunities.

Subject + Base form of verb (+s/es for 3rd singular)

Do/does + subject + Base form of verb

Subject + do/does + not + Base form of verb

_ _ _ _____I_____ _ _ _
   Now

PRESENT CONTINUOUS

I AM CLEANING

(Action taking place at time of speaking)

Context: It's 11 a.m. and we are attending one of Sally's sessions

Sally is welcoming the audience.

She is introducing herself to us.

Now she is smiling to someone in the first row who probably has asked for her autograph.

Now she is writing something on the board.

Subject + Am/are/is + -ing form

Am/are/is + subject + -ing form

Subject + Am/are/is + not + -ing form

_ _ _ ___IIIII _____ _ _

Now

Be careful! Some verbs cannot be generally used in the continuous form. Some of them are like, love, want, know, understand, depend, prefer, remember, hate, mean, believe, forget. They require the Present simple.

Grammar exercises

1. Check the correct form of the present (simple or continuous):

1. At the moment we (analyse/are analysing) the situation and we will soon be able to give an answer to stakeholders

2. I (am seeing/see) my clients most afternoons

3. The sun (sets/is setting) in the west

4. I can't help you right now. (I'm talking/talk) on the phone with a client.

5. I (don't usually have/am not usually having) a coffee but I (have/am having) one this morning because there is nothing else

6. Where is Ben? I think (he is smoking/smokes) a cigarette

7. The Robinsons are in New York at last. They (are staying/stay) at the Royal Palace.

8. (I'm not liking/don't like) this kind of music. It horrifies me.

9. (I believe/am believing) in the power of self-motivation

10. I don't understand what (you say/are saying)! What (do you mean/are you meaning) by lack of enthusiasm?

2. Answer the following questions (in writing):

1. What do you do?
2. What does your job involve?
3. What time do you usually get to work (university)?
4. Do you go to work by bus or by car?
5. How often do you eat out at lunch?
6. When do you finish work (studying)?
7. How often do you watch TV after dinner?
8. How many hours do you sleep a day?
9. Where do you have breakfast?
10. Do you read a newspaper every day?

3. Choose the correct form: present simple or present continuous

The housing crisis

England (1) suffers/is suffering a massive housing crisis. There simply aren't enough decent, affordable homes.

- More than two million people (2) find/are finding their rent or mortgage a constant struggle or (3) fall/are falling behind with payments.

- Against a background of mounting debt across the country, huge numbers of homeowners (4) have/are having their homes repossessed, because they are no longer able to keep up with their mortgage repayments.

- Second home ownership (5) is pricing/prices local people out of many rural areas.

- Over 1.7 million households (6) are currently waiting/wait for social housing.

- Some homeless households - many with dependent children – (7) wait/are waiting for years in temporary accommodation.

- Families renting privately on low incomes (8) are having/have to put up with poor living conditions and little security.

- The number of new households (9) increases/is increasing faster than the number of house builds.

- And at the sharpest end, many hundreds of people (10) sleep/are sleeping rough on the streets every night, cold and fearing for their safety.

Shelter (11) is believing/believes this situation is unacceptable.

4. Rewrite words containing possible mistakes:

1. I had never though about it before

2. You will achieve your target thorough hard work and commitment

3. People should be honest and straightforward. I don't like people who don't tell the true

4. The trough is that you don't want to work hard

5. Even thought she is a good employee she spends much time at the coffee machine

6. When the going gets thought, the thought get going

Chapter 9
PEOPLE JOBS

Pre-reading activity A

Before reading the article below, answer the following question:

How important is a career in your life?

_____

After having a look at the glossary below, move on to the reading activity:

GLOSSARY:

English word/phrase	English equivalent or definition
Prospect	Future possibility, chance of something beneficial
To hold true	To be true, to remain true
Healthcare	Medical services
To deem	To judge or consider, to view as
Tissue	A part of an organism with a large number of

	cells having a similar structure
Gene	Unit of DNA
To highlight	O emphasize
Elderly	Old; *the elderly* means old people
To age	To grow older
Maid	Domestic servant
To yield	To produce
Coach	A trainer or instructor; tutor

Reading activity A

Best Careers for the Future - what is the best future job career?

Many websites will try to tell you which careers offer the best prospects for the future. Their choices are usually based on percentage growth statistics for recent years, which are a clear indicator of where the numbers of jobs are increasing.

However, this does not reflect other concerns such as which careers pay best, which jobs are easiest to obtain, which need the longest periods of undergraduate and postgraduate study, and so on. Despite this, some general trends hold true on a general level.

Future career trends

It is no surprise that one of the fastest growing areas of employment in recent years relates to computer technology. Technological advance and the continued integration of IT and digital communications into the workplace throughout the private, public and voluntary sectors ensures that this trend will continue for some time. Systems analysts, designers and developers, computer programmers, web developers, consultants and information managers reflect the range of these career areas. Hardware engineers are also needed, working in infrastructure construction and repair, fibre, cable, satellites, etc.

Another guaranteed growth area is the healthcare sector. The increasing number of healthcare jobs is directly attributable to the growing age of the population – people are living longer so there are more people in the older age groups – and the expansion of treatments available for medical conditions, whether delivered in the primary healthcare sector or within hospitals. Consequently, there is also an expansion in the number of administrative and support roles needing to be filled.

Other careers deemed to be 'hot' future career prospects relate to areas of scientific advance, and in particular the "bio" sciences, such as biotechnology. Tissue engineers and gene programmers have been highlighted, but all skill levels are included – as companies grow, so does their administration infrastructure. Other new scientific areas include nanotechnology and energy technology.

Demographic changes are leading to other needs in addition to healthcare. Teaching and tourism, training and development, and care of the elderly are all areas where openings are set to increase, as are financial advisors.

Services that already exist will grow further as the population ages. Standard professions include the legal sector, police, teachers, tutors, etc. Meanwhile, there is a general return amongst certain income sectors of paying for domestic support with the services of maids and cleaners, drivers, etc. This is increasingly common as the higher divorce levels yield more one-parent families.

New services are developing that are opening out into recognized career fields. Many of these are provided directly to the consumer. Counselling and various complementary therapies are obvious examples, as well as physical training instructors and coaches.

Post-reading activity A 1 (Comprehension)

Answer the following questions about the article:

1. How do most websites provide you information about the best job careers?

2. Is there any information that is often neglected by these types of websites?

3. Are there good prospects of employment in computer technology?

4. Why is the healthcare sector increasing?

5. Are there any 'hot' careers in science?

6. Why is the area of domestic support likely to grow?

Post-reading activity A 2 (Vocabulary)

Match the words on the left to their definitions on the right:

A. Systems analyst   1. Develop, design, and test various computer equipment.

B. Web developer   2. Prevents and detects crime, and maintains public order.

C. Hardware engineer   3. Researches problems, plans solutions, recommends software and systems

D. Policeman   4. Provides education for pupils and students

E. Tissue engineer   5. Guides or advises but he/she can also be a talk therapist

F. Financial advisor   6. Cleans homes or offices for payment

G. Teacher   7. Repairs or replaces parts of or whole tissues (bone, blood vessels, skin, muscle etc.).

H. Cleaner   8. Renders financial services to clients (brokers, investment advisers, accountants, insurance agents and financial planners)

I. Counsellor   9. Is a programmer who specialises in the development of World Wide Web applications

Post-reading activity A 3 (Speaking)

Explain the meaning of the following quote and say whether you agree or not:

"Choose a job you love, and you will never have to work a day in your life." – Confucius

Grammar revision

FUTURE SIMPLE

I WILL CLEAN

(Action decided at the time of speaking; predictions; offering, promising or asking to do something)

The future simple is often associated with: probably, (I) think, (I) don't think, (I) am sure, (I) wonder

Technological advance ensures that this trend will continue for some time.

Services that already exist will grow further as the population ages.

Many websites will try to tell you which careers offer the best prospects for the future

Perhaps as many as three stores will be open by the end of the first year

By not giving your full attention to the team, they will feel second rate and less motivated.

Avoiding these common traps will help business leaders create lasting motivation for their teams

If you don't have objectives you often won't produce anything

Maybe I will be successful, maybe I will not.

Subject + will ('ll) + Base form of verb

Will + Subject + Base form of verb

Subject + will + not (won't) + Base form of verb

There are other forms to express the future in English depending on the nuance of meaning you want to give to the sentence:

PRESENT CONTINUOUS

We have arranged to do something, to go somewhere, to meet someone (personal arrangements):

He's meeting some clients tomorrow evening

I'm not working tomorrow so we can go to the mall.

He's leaving tomorrow at 6 am for Milan

PRESENT SIMPLE

We talk about programmes and timetables (public transport, TV shows, concerts). We also use the present simple when people's plans are fixed like timetables:

The plane leaves at 6.30 from Gatwick airport.

The concert starts at 8.30 pm

It's Sunday tomorrow

I finish my swimming lesson at 7 tomorrow.

TO BE GOING TO

We use this form when we have decided (but not arranged) to do something, we intend to do something:

I'm going to talk to Susan tomorrow. Today she looked a little disappointed.

There's an interesting documentary on TV this evening. Are you going to watch it?

Your car is really old and unsafe! – Yes, I'm going to buy a new one soon

Reading activity B

Executive Assistant

Employer: Noxam Group Ltd.

Posted: 8 January 2013

Location: Central London

Function: Secretarial

Contract: Permanent

Hours: Full Time

Salary: £23,000

JOB ADVERT

Are you fond of the arts, culture and luxury brands?

Do you have proven office management, client relationship and research skills?

Can you respond to a fast paced, entrepreneurial and varied work environment?

Do you have first-rate organisational, administrative and communication skills?

Are you keen to transfer these skills and experience to a boutique consultancy with a strong arts focus?

ABOUT US

Founded in 2001, Noxam Group is an independent business that creates high-level alliances between global corporations and world-class cultural institutions and artists. We serve our clients by designing and implementing inventive campaigns that provide major return on investment. Across our work, our core knowledge lies in strategy and organisational development, the creation of unique brand development partnerships, and the establishment of long-term, sustainable income generation.

THE OPPORTUNITY

We are seeking a professional with established experience of office administration, diary management, research and client relationship management relating to arts, management consulting, financial services, luxury brands or consumer goods. The person will predominantly support the Managing Director in all aspects of her work, including personal administration and philanthropic activity. You will also support Noxam Group's business development processes, including researching target clients and attending meetings and pitches. You will be supporting a small, active team to deliver for corporate and cultural clients.

THE PERSON

Qualified with a strong track record in office administration with excellent written and oral communications skills. You will have a strong interest in marketing, brand and communications, with a good understanding of both the corporate and cultural world. You need to be adaptable, able to think on your feet and show initiative. You will be a first rate communicator and be able to engage confidently with clients and artists. Goal orientated, you will be at ease working as part of a small company in a fast paced environment that has a strong team spirit.

A passion for the arts is essential.

Post-reading activity B 1 (Comprehension)

Answer the following questions about the job advert:

1. Which skills are required in the job advert?
2. What does the Company do?
3. Which opportunities are offered by Noxam Group?
4. What kind of person are they looking for?

Post-reading activity B 2 (Speaking)

Study the candidates' profiles below and then discuss with your classmates about the best employee for Noxam. Practice each possible solution as you role-play with your classmates:

Candidate	Mary Sutter	Consuelo Esteban	Jane Leserman
Age	32	29	43
Marital status	Divorced, 1 child	Single	Married, two children
Qualifications	BA, Business Administration	BA (Hons), History of Art	MBA, Business Administration BA, European Studies

| Experience | CSZ Business cons., London, Head of Administration

Planning and co-ordinating the administration Providing general office management

Ensuring that the office records, databases and information systems are well maintained and protected Overseeing personnel, health and safety policies, security and any other non-financial policies/procedures | Sushi Gallery

Event planner

Assisting with all corporate or event planning needs

Discussing, arranging and co-ordinating any plans or ideas that potential clients may have for their functions

Managing product launches, fashion shows or awards ceremonies for clients | Christine Lauder

Regional educator

Building education programs and systems, delivering these throughout the network. Public speaking, motivating teams to reach company goals and objectives. |
|---|---|---|---|
| Skills | Computing

Driving

Communication and planning | Communication

Planning activities

Drawing

Musical instruments (piano) | Bookkeeping

Organize diaries, itineraries and meetings

Public speaking |
Languages	--	Mother tongue Spanish	Fluent in French
I.Q. Test	Above average	Average	Average
Notes	**Sometimes takes days off without notice**	--	**Self centred**

Supplementary activity

How to write a good cv

A good cv is needed when you are looking for a job. A well written curriculum vitae will help you make you more visible and possibly get that interview you are eager to have. Here you will find advice on how to structure your cv, without leaving out important details and filling it with useless information just to use space.

Personal details

Work experience

Achievements

Education

Hobbies and interests

References

Grammar exercises

1. Read the following sentences and then add them to the table below:

1. I think the economy will recover by the end of this year

2. I'm going to study Russian next year since it is a very important language.

3. We're flying to Moscow on Monday.

4. Are you going to leave the company this year?

5. John is going to leave tonight

6. The train leaves at 5

7. Our Chinese boss is visiting us this Easter

8. Do you think the company will close down?

9. Next year I'm going to stop smoking

10. She will probably be promoted and given a pay rise

Function	Which sentence above?	Name of tense
We have arranged to do something, to go somewhere, to		

meet someone (personal arrangements)		
We talk about programmes and timetables (public transport, TV shows, concerts).		
We decide sth. at the time of speaking; we make predictions; we offer to do sth., we promise or ask to do sth.		
We use this form when we have decided (but not arranged) to do sth., we intend to do sth.		

2. Fill in the gaps with the correct future tense:

1) The bus _____ at 9:35. (to pass)

2) I _____ dinner with Susan on Saturday. (to have)

3) It _____ in the Apennines in the weekend. (to snow)

4) On Friday at 10.30 I _____ my cousin. (to meet)

5) He _____ to Berlin on Monday morning. (to fly)

6) Don't worry! I _____ you to the station. (to take)

7) The film _____ at 9:15. (to start)

9) I don't think it_____. (to rain)

10) You look busy! I _____ the phone for you. (to answer)

Supplementary activity 1 (Listening)

You can find many examples of job interviews on the internet. If you go to Youtube you will be able to find many and it will be a very good exercise to improve your listening skills. Moreover, you will be able to learn some useful tips to be used when having a job interview. You could start from the following:

"Job Interview Tips & Techniques: How to Prepare for a First Impression"

"Job Interview Tips - Job Interview Questions and Answers"

"How To Find A Job During A Recession"

Chapter 10
COMPANIES TRENDS

Pre-reading activity A

A trend is a tendency. The word is very common in business to describe downward and upward directions of the economy, sales, profits and other elements. Before reading the article below, have a look at what linguists call strong collocations, i.e. combinations of words which are often associated to one another:

Market trend(s)

Business trend(s)

Economic trend(s)

Price trend(s)

Employment trend(s)

Trend analysis

Inflationary trend

If something is unclear you can easily search for information on the net. Now move on to the glossary and afterwards read the article given below.

GLOSSARY:

English word/phrase	English equivalent or definition
Groundhog	A woodchuck
Mast	A vertical spar for supporting sails and flags on a vessel
Pesky	Causing trouble
Hat tip	Congratulations, *chapeau*
Notch	A step or level
Doldrums	Depressed condition, sadness; *econ.* A period of slow economy
Come	By
Brit	*Inf.* A British person
Dependable	Reliable
Household	People who live in one house collectively; *adj.* domestic
To account for	To be the total of
Spike	Peak
Wedged	Squeezed into a narrow space
Rut	A predictable way of life, routine
Stuck	Unable to move

Groundhog Day is a day celebrated in America and Canada on 2 February. On that day the small animal is said to get out of its burrow if the day is cloudy and to retreat back inside if it is sunny, as in this case it would be frightened by its own shadow. From the groundhog's behaviour people would be able to know whether the spring will come early or if winter will still continue. The 1993 American comedy starring Bill Murray and Andy McDowell is about a self-centred weatherman who covering the Groundhog Day event, relives a single day over and over again. So, when you say "It's Groundhog Day" you feel a sense of deja vu, as though the exact same thing had happened before.

Reading activity A

Inflation stands at 2.7%. Again

It's like Groundhog Day over at the Office for National Statistics. Inflation has remained unchanged for the third month in a row.

Ah, inflation. Every month, just like the last, on her ship tied to the mast. According to the ONS, the consumer prices index in December remained at 2.7%.

Why is it not falling, you ask? Ah, it'll be those pesky hikes in energy prices. Electricity prices were up 3.9% compared with December 2011, while gas prices were 5.2% higher.

Without those extra pounds added to the cost of living, falling petrol prices (down 0.2% - hat tip to the Coalition for cancelling that fuel rise) and air transport costs (down 6.8%), could have taken inflation down a notch or two.

These inflationary doldrums are bad news for the Bank of England. We're still no closer to the mythical target of 2%, promised to us since late 2009. And we'll be in the same boat come January if the price of food and drink keeps on rising. Still we're a few leagues away from that terrifying inflationary peak of 5.2%, so that's something.

Your average Brit is still out of pocket however. According to the latest data on average earnings, released in October, wages have risen just 1.3%. This leaves the consumer-led recovery looking less and less dependable. MT wonders if the Office for Budget Responsibility will be forced to rethink its forecast that household consumption will account for 0.5% of the UK's 1.2% economic growth this year...

If you can raise the deposit, it's a good time to buy a house though. In real terms (CPI-adjusted) UK house prices are 22% lower than they were in August 2007 (just 10% lower in London, however).

So what do the wise heads from the worlds of economics and finance predict for inflation in the coming months? Sarah Hewin, head of research at Standard Chartered, says: 'The outlook I think is probably for inflation falling, rather than inflation rising.' Victoria Clarke, an economist at Investec, counters with, 'Inflation will rise above 3% over the coming months.' Commerzbank economist Peter Dixon adds, 'It's entirely possible that by mid-year we'll get a very sharp spike in inflation back above 3%.'

So, nobody really knows, then? If inflation remains stubbornly high, policy makers at the MPC will shy away from further quantitative easing. With our economy wedged firmly in a growth rut, that leaves us all, just like Bill Murray, stuck in Groundhog Day.

Post-reading activity A 1 (Comprehension)

Answer the following questions about the article:

1. Has inflation increased or decreased in the last three months in Britain?

2. To what does the author attribute the current situation of inflation?

3. Why should the Bank of England be unhappy with the situation?

4. Have British wages risen more than inflation?

5. Why does the author think it is a good moment to buy houses?

6. Are the forecasts for inflation in the next few months contradictory?

7. Why does the author compare British stable inflation to the movie Groundhog Day starring Bill Murray?

Post-reading activity A 2 (Speaking)

Have a look at the verbs below. They describe upward, downward and steady trends. Then work on the chart about UK inflation rate and describe the phenomenon based on the data given:

Verbs describing general upward movement

Go up – increase – rise – ascend – grow

Verbs describing rapid upward movement

Rocket – soar

Verbs describing general downward movement

Go down – fall – drop – descend – decline

Verbs describing rapid downward movement

Plummet

Verbs describing steady trend

Stay the same – remain constant – stagnate (negative)

Verbs describing the reaching of a stable trend

Flatten out – level off

Verbs describing a very high level

Hit a peak – peak

Verbs describing a very low level

Hit a low – bottom out

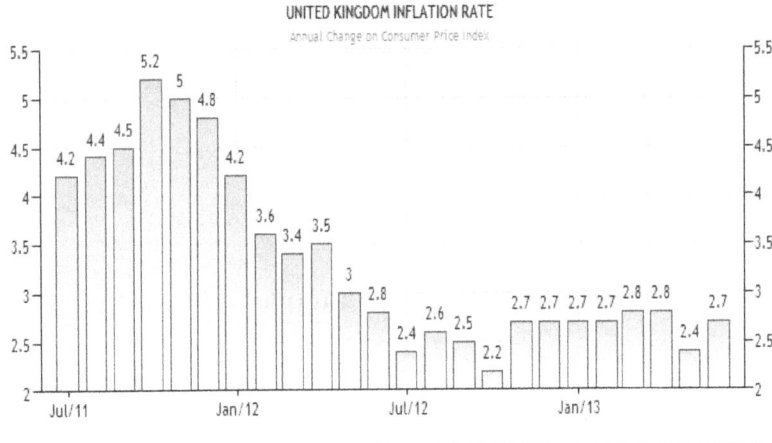

Verbs describing trends may be modified by adverbs that can adjust the meaning of the verbs used. For ex. We can say profits fell last year but we can be more precise by saying profits fell dramatically last year. Of course we can also use prepositions to talk about figures, such as in profits fell by 5.3% last year.

The most common adverbs used to express trends are the following:

Rapidly – sharply – drastically – dramatically – slightly – gradually – slowly – moderately

The most common prepositions used to express changes and define them are the following:

By – at – of – in – from...to

Post-reading activity A 3 (Comprehension)

Read the following article and put the words in brackets into the correct form (verbs, adjectives and nouns). As for preposition decide which one fits best in the text:

Rents 'fall for third month in row'

Rents 1. (fall: verb) _____ by 0.3pc month-on-month to reach £732 per month on average, taking them back to levels seen in July last year, according to LSL Property Services. Recent lending figures have shown increases in first-time buyer numbers following the introduction of Government schemes aiming to give people a leg up onto the property ladder.

The rental dip seen for the last three months has followed 2. (soar: adjective) _____ rents due to high numbers of would-be buyers who have found themselves trapped in renting because they have not been able to get access to a mortgage.

The number of mortgages on the market has increased 3. (preposition)_____ around one third and lenders have been offering some of their lowest ever rates since the Government's Funding for Lending scheme to help borrowers was introduced last August.

The latest LSL study found that the South East saw the 4. (sharp: adjective) _____ monthly fall 5. (preposition)_____ rents, with a 1.5pc drop taking average rents to £744. The East Midlands saw the strongest monthly 6. (increase: noun) _____, with a 1.2pc 7. (rise: noun) _____ pushing typical rents to £547.

Rents dipped 8. (preposition)_____ 0.2pc month-on-month in London, although at £1,086 on average they are still 5.2pc higher than a year ago.

Overall, rents across England and Wales are 2.8pc higher year-on-year, and the rate of the recent spate of falls 9. (slow: verb) _____ in January, suggesting that rents are poised for another upward march, the study said.

David Newnes, director of LSL Property Services, said: "An improving mortgage market in January helped take a little pressure off the limited supply of 10. (rent: noun) _____ property, at a time when demand from tenants on the move is far from its seasonal peaks.

"But the dip in competition is not likely to last long.

"The pace of the fall 11. (preposition)_____ monthly rents has slowed, and we're already seeing tenant activity pick up. "The private rented sector is coiled for a spring bounce."

Figures from the Council of Mortgage Lenders (CML) showed yesterday that buy-to-let lending 12. (grow: verb) _____ by a fifth year-on-year across 2012 to reach its highest level since 2008.

The LSL study also found that tenant arrears had improved compared with the costly Christmas period of December.

Some 8.1pc of rent across England and Wales was late or unpaid in January, compared with 10.1pc in December.

Reading activity B

What went wrong in Greece?

After months of refusing to accept the idea of Greece leaving the euro, eurozone politicians are slowly beginning to acknowledge there may be no option but to let the country go.

Why is Greece in trouble?

Greece was living beyond its means even before it joined the euro. After it adopted the single currency, public spending soared. Public sector wages, for example, rose 50% between 1999 and 2007 - far faster than in other eurozone countries.

And while money flowed out of the government's coffers, its income was hit by widespread tax evasion. So, after years of overspending, its budget deficit - the difference between spending and income - spiralled out of control. When the global financial downturn hit, therefore, Greece was ill-prepared to cope.

Debt levels reached the point where the country was no longer able to repay its loans, and was forced to ask for help from its European partners and the International Monetary Fund (IMF) in the form of massive loans. In the short term, however, the conditions attached to these loans have compounded Greece's woes.

Post-reading activity B 1 (Comprehension)

The list below contains synonyms of some words of the article. Read the text again and complete:

Expenditure

_____

Huge

_____

Admit

    Acknowledge_____

Slump

_____

To pay back

_____

Increased

_____

Exacerbated

_____

Extensive

_____

Resources

_____

Extravagance

_____

Torment

_____

Alternative

_____

Manage

_____

Treasury

_____

Salaries

_____

Post-reading activity B 2 (Speaking)

Discuss the following statement:

"I try not to borrow, first you borrow then you beg." Ernest Hemingway, writer

Supplementary activity 1 (Listening)

Good exercises for practicing the language of graphs and trends are available on Youtube. One of them is "How to Describe Graphs and Trends in English".

Chapter 11
ACTIVITIES DISCUSSING ISSUES

When you wish to discuss something you should be able to express your ideas clearly and orderly. Below you will find some useful examples of ways to express opinions, preferences, agreement and disagreement (See Unit 5 Post-reading activity B 3). Remember that expressions are more polite and formal than others, so adjust them to the context:

Opinions and preferences:

I think..., In my opinion..., I'd like to..., I'd rather..., I'd prefer..., The way I see it..., As far as I'm concerned..., If it were up to me..., I suppose..., I suspect that..., I'm pretty sure that..., It is fairly certain that..., I'm convinced that..., I honestly feel that..., I strongly believe that..., Without a doubt,...

Expressing agreement with an opinion:

Yes/yeah. ...Exactly/quite/absolutely/definitely. ...Right/ All right// Yes you're right. ...That's (quite) right/true. ...Quite so. ...Of course. ...Yes/well I suppose so. ...I agree (entirely)./ ...I think so, too. ...I couldn't agree more. ...That's just exactly what I think/thought/ was thinking. ...That's what I was going to say. ....You took the words out of my mouth! ...That's a good point. ... So/neither do I/ Me too.

Disagreeing:

I don't think that..., Don't you think it would be better..., I don't agree, I'd prefer..., Shouldn't we consider..., But what about..., I'm afraid I don't agree..., Frankly, I doubt if..., Let's face it, the truth of the matter is..., The problem with your point of view is that...

Brainstorming is used in many companies as it generates ideas. The employees' ideas do not receive any criticism. The activity is usually divided into three phases. Participants just provide ideas that could lead to the solution of a problem.

First, they decide on the topic to consider. The group will generate words and phrases that come to their mind and someone will write them on a board.

Second, ideas should be taken and organised. For example, similar ideas, just worded differently, should be combined into one idea.

The third phase consists in examining the list and discarding the ideas that are not practical, feasible or that are contradictory. What remains should be arranged in order of importance, feasibility and affordability.

A similar method could be used in language learning in order to develop vocabulary and improve conversation skills.

EXAMPLE

Problem: Our planet is increasingly polluted and congested. How could this problem be solved?

To the teacher: The first step should aim to identify words related to pollution (nouns, adjectives, acronyms, verbs and so on). This will greatly help students to face the discussion phase, so start asking what to write on the board. Set the time deadline for the class (ex. 10 mins.)

Harmful

Dangerous

Damaging

- Tougher laws
- Effects
- Air
- Water
- Land
- To destroy
- The ozone layer
- Gases
- Radiations
- Global warming
- Carbon dioxide
- Acid rain
- Chemicals
- International agreements
- Smoke
- Factories
- The greens
- Conservation
- Protection
- Exhaust fumes

Industrial waste

To throw away

Spray

To cut down

Tropical rainforests

To recycle

To plant

Natural resources

To set up

Natural parks

Now ask the group if they know the words and phrases on the board and divide them into different areas (grammar, causes and effects, etc.):

Adjectives	Environment	Causes of pollution	Remedies	Verbs
Harmful	Air	The ozone layer	The greens	To destroy
Dangerous	Water	Gases	Conservation	To throw away

Damaging	Land	Radiations	Protection	To cut down
	Tropical rainforests	Global warming	Tougher laws	To recycle
	Natural resources	Carbon dioxide	Agreements	To plant
		Acid rain	Natural parks	To set up
		Chemicals		
		Smoke		
		Factories		
		Exhaust fumes		
		Industrial waste		
		Spray		

Conversation

Conversation is an interactive form of communication involving two or more people who are supposed to follow rules of good manners. Someone says that conversation is an art and probably it is so, because according to the basic principles of communication we communicate with other people in order to reach our goals. This means that also in everyday conversation we try to persuade other people. But whatever the purpose it may serve, follow the rules below:

- Be natural
- Listen more than you talk
- Adapt the conversation to the listener
- Respect the turn-taking rules
- Think before speaking
- Do not interrupt
- Do not talk to only one person if you are in a group
- Do not over-share your life

Now you are ready to start a conversation the conversation. Make sure you use the words and phrases you have just learned. The following exercise could be a good test for practicing your students' speaking skills. It should be done in pairs or in bigger groups, in order to make different opinions come out and encourage the use of the above words:

- University is useless because young people do not learn a job. They study subjects no employers want and then they cannot find a job.

- Patience is an innate quality. You cannot learn how to become more patient and if you can how do you learn to behave patiently?

- Men and women are equal at last but women continue to earn considerably less than men and can't break the glass ceiling in their companies.

- Violence in the media needs to be regulated. Children's programmes should be appropriate for their ages and stages of development.

- Most private sector workers think the public sector has it better as regards job security, training, holidays and equal opportunities.

- When you speak a foreign language 50% of your communicative skills get lost because of anxiety and fear.

- We are what we want to be and happiness lies in our own hands!

- Problem-solving is the first skill you need to have in a managerial position

- Money, then health and thirdly love are the things that count most in life, in order of importance

- Speaking on the phone in English is really embarrassing

- Clients are the most important source of life a company has, so they are always right

- A Two-speed Europe may be inevitable economically

- Can Italy still afford its health care system or paying for a private insurance, like in the U.S. should be taken into consideration?

- European soccer has become an industrial-system of corruption, a wrong business model which is no longer based on values but only on money

Chapter 12
ACTIVITIES DESCRIBING PEOPLE AND THINGS

One common situation when speaking English is having to describe something or someone or asking questions to know about something or someone. This may either be a person or a thing, and in both cases we should be familiar with question words and adjectives. The verb to be will be extremely important too

Look at picture 1. You don't know the man portrayed so you might ask some typical questions such as:

What's his name? His name is John Tennet

How old is he?	He's 63 (years old)
What does he do?	He's an entrepreneur
What is he like?	He's very kind and friendly
Where is he from?	He's from Norwich
When was he born?	He was born in 1950
Where was he born?	He was born in London

Suppose you are talking to a friend about his boss and you don't know exactly if you have ever met him. You could ask your him some questions to get some more details which might help you remember. You could ask?

What does he look like?	He's quite tall and corpulent
How tall is he?	He's (about) 1 m 78
How much does he weigh?	He weighs (approximately) 85 kg

Remember: when we ask about someone's character and personality we say What is he/she/Mr Brown like? When we want to know about someone's physical traits we say What does he/she/Mrs Doodley look like?

Physical features

Attractive

Bald

Beautiful

Blonde

Curly (hair)

Dark haired

Dark skinned

Fair-haired

Fat

Fit

Flabby

Good looking

Gorgeous

Handsome

Large

Medium build

Medium height

Muscular

Obese

Plain

Scruffy

Short

Skinny

Slender

Slim

Smart

Stout

Straight (hair)

Tall

Tanned

Thin

Wavy (hair)

Well-built

Psychological features (positive)

adaptable

adventurous

affable

affectionate

agreeable

ambitious

amusing

brave

bright

broad-minded

calm

careful

charming

convivial

creative

decisive

determined

diligent

diplomatic

discreet

easygoing

emotional

enthusiastic

extroverted

faithful

frank

funny

generous

hard-working

helpful

honest

impartial

intelligent

intuitive

inventive

kind

loyal

modest

optimistic

passionate

patient

pioneering

polite

powerful

practical

pro-active

quiet

rational

reliable

reserved

resourceful

self-confident

sensible

sensitive

shy

sincere

sympathetic

tidy

tough

versatile

willing

witty

Psychological features (negative)

aggressive

arrogant

boastful

boring

bossy

changeable

compulsive

conservative

cowardly

cruel

cynical

deceitful

detached

dishonest

domineering

flirtatious

fussy

greedy

gullible

impatient

impolite

impulsive

inconsistent

indecisive

indiscreet

inflexible

interfering

intolerant

introverted

lazy

machiavellian

materialistic

mean

moody

narrow-minded

nervous

obsessive

obstinate

overcritical

pessimistic

pompous

quarrelsome

resentful

rude

ruthless

sarcastic

selfish

self-centred

silly

stingy

stubborn

superficial

tactless

touchy

unreliable

untidy

vague

vengeful

vulgar

Exercise:

Fill in the blanks with the required word or one which make sense:

1)

Andrew   -My girlfriend's name is Sarah.

Bob   -What _____ like?

Andrew -She is _____, well... good-looking! She is tall and _____.

Bob   -How _____ is she?

Andrew -She is about 1 metre 70.

Bob   -_____ does she weigh?

Andrew -This is not a kind question for a woman! Anyway, she _____ about 50 Kilos. She's fair-_____. Her hair _____ long and curly. She has blue eyes.

2)

Anna   -This morning we met our new managing director.

Brenda - Did you? And what's he _____?

Anna   - As a matter of fact, he just stayed few minutes with us, but I got quite a good impression of him. He looks _____ and friendly, _____ and easy-going.

Brenda - So, nothing to do with Mr. Robertson, your old boss. He was so _____ and unkind. He was _____, nervous and even looked miserable.

Activity 1 (Speaking)

Work in pairs and take turns answering the following questions:

1. What are your main qualities?

2. What are your main flaws?

3. What are the qualities you appreciate the most in a person?

4. What are the qualities you appreciate the most in a friend/colleague/boss?

5. What are the worst flaws in a person?

6. Do you think you could eliminate your flaws? If so, by doing what?

7. Turn the following adjectives into nouns: ex. brave > bravery

Attractive – diplomatic – patient – versatile – stubborn – dishonest – unreliable – stout – sincere – optimist – cruel – kind

Activity 2 (Reading/Speaking)

Read the opinions posted on our website about successful entrepreneurs. You will notice that people use a lot of adjectives to describe the characteristics needed to become one of them. Underline both positive and negative adjectives:

As far as I see it, a good entrepreneur ought to be creative, enthusiastic and adventurous. I think you have to be ambitious, determined and intuitive. You also need vision for doing business and above all passion. (Jane, 1969)

I am convinced that an entrepreneur is made and not born. Entrepreneurs are highly motivated men and women in the sense of achieving targets. Money is not necessarily what motivates them, but it is very important. These people, I mean...good entrepreneurs also have a strong sense of initiative and like doing things on their own rather than involve other people. They are dedicated to their businesses and put as much time into them as they can. They work for themselves rather than for anyone else. They know the market very well and have strokes of genius. (Eddie, 1980)

I guess there are more than a few reasons that make someone a good entrepreneur. They are supposed to be motivated by their desire for moving up the ladder. Their life is not easy since they have to be hard-working and very pro-active.

An entrepreneur has to be very goal driven as well, so they need to be organized. (Rachel, 1977)

If I were to open my own business and become an entrepreneur I am sure I would learn very soon that you need to network. Yes, networking is decisive. Of course I might encounter deceitful people, as well as quarrelsome and intolerant ones. Well, I don't like being influenced...I'm neither naive nor gullible; of course there is nothing wrong with taking advice or opinions, in the end, but you must make decisions by yourself. (Sam, 1971)

Luck is not the reason why entrepreneurs become successful. Every successful entrepreneur is usually intelligent, creative and intuitive. As business models are constantly changing. Of course they have to be ready to change, I'd say adaptable, versatile. I think the most successful entrepreneurs know how fast trends change and they can anticipate what they will be like in the short term. (Peter, 1965)

Reading activity

Those are my principles

You and I have principles. And we also have opinions. I have opinions about what I think is right or wrong or good or bad. But they're only opinions - I COULD be wrong! I won't try to build my life around my opinions, but I WILL endeavor to stand by my principles.

A 15-year-old boy learned a valuable lesson about life principles. He wrote a letter to "Dear Abby" about finding a woman's wallet that contained $127 as well as the woman's identification. He hopped onto his bicycle and peddled over to her house - about a mile away. He told her he found her wallet and she gave him a big hug. She also gave him twenty dollars.

That evening the boy told his parents about the event and his father said, "I don't think you should have accepted $20 for doing what you should have done. A person shouldn't be rewarded for being honest."

He pondered his father's statement and decided he would return the money. He biked to the lady's home and gave her back the twenty dollars. She didn't want to take it, but he told her she had to - that his father pointed out something to him that he had never realized before. Her eyes filled with tears as she said, "This is one for Ripley."

The boy's question to Abby? "Abby, who is Ripley?"

Is a life built around principles so unusual that Robert Ripley should mention it in his column "Believe It or Not"? When ideals such as honesty and a personal standard of always doing the right thing guide our every action and decision, we actually change. These great principles shape our lives and make us into persons of character. They build self esteem and teach confidence. That boy is fortunate to be raised by a wise father who had the wisdom to say, "Those are my principles."

Martin Luther King, Jr. put it well: "The time is always right to do what is right." Those were his principles. Decide to always do what is right - today and every day - and you will find yourself building a life that matters.

From http://halife.com/inspiring/principles.html by Steve Goodier

Notes to the text

- Dear Abby is the name of an advice column run by a woman who dispenses advice and maternal wisdom. It is undoubtedly the most popular column in the world.

- The sentence This is one for Ripley refers to Ripley's Believe It or Not! It is a newspaper column, radio show, and television show, founded by Robert Ripley, about bizarre and unusual events from around the world.

Post-reading activity (Writing)

Answer the following questions:

1. Can you find three adjectives to describe the boy in the story?

2. What did he do after finding the wallet?

3. How did the woman react when she received her wallet back?

4. What did the boy's father say about the reward his son had been given?

5. Why did the lady said that the boy was one for Ripley?

6. What is the author's idea about the story?

Appendix 1
List of irregular verbs

beat - beat - beaten

become - became - become

begin - began - begun

bend - bent - bent

bite - bit - bitten

blow - blew - blown

break - broke - broken

bring - brought - brought

build - built - built

burst - burst - burst

buy - bought - bought

catch - caught - caught

choose - chose - chosen

come - came - come

cost - cost - cost

cut - cut - cut

dig - dug - dug

do - did - done

draw - drew - drawn

drink - drank - drunk

drive - drove - driven

eat - ate - eaten

fall - fell - fallen

feed - fed - fed

feel - felt - felt

fight - fought - fought

find - found - found

fly - flew - flown

forget - forgot - forgotten

freeze - froze - frozen

give - gave - given

go - went - gone

grow - grew - grown

have - had - had

hear - heard - heard

hide - hid - hidden

hit - hit - hit

hold - held - held

hurt - hurt - hurt

keep - kept - kept

know - knew - known

lead - led - led

leave - left - left   let - let - let

light - lit - lit

lose - lost - lost

make - made - made

mean - meant - meant

meet - met - met

pay - paid - paid

put - put - put

read - read - read

ride - rode - ridden

ring - rang - rung

rise - rose - risen

run - ran - run

say - said - said

see - saw - seen

sell - sold - sold

send - sent - sent

shake - shook - shaken

shine - shone - shone

shoot - shot - shot

shut - shut - shut

sing - sang - sung

sink - sank - sunk

sit - sat - sat

sleep - slept - slept

speak - spoke - spoken

spread - spread - spread

stand - stood - stood

steal - stole - stolen

stick - stuck - stuck

strike - struck - struck

sweep - swept - swept

swim - swam - swum

take - took - taken

teach - taught - taught

tear - tore - torn

tell - told - told

think - thought - thought

throw - threw - thrown

wake - woke - woken

wear - wore - worn

win - won - won

write - wrote - written

Appendix 2
Idioms, sayings and proverbs

An idiom is a group of words whose meaning considered as a whole is different from the meanings of each word considered separately. A typical example of idiomatic forms are phrasal verbs, but the altered meaning of combinations of a group of words is also evident in sayings and proverbs. Look at the list below and try to explain the meaning of the expressions given with your own words:

SAYINGS AND PROVERBS

It's better to be idiot than to pretend wise

A good enemy is a better person than a false friend

An apple a day keeps the doctor away.

A bad workman (always) blames his tools.

A banker is someone who lends you an umbrella when the sun is shining, and who asks for it back when it starts to rain.

A bargain is something you don't need at a price you can't resist.

A bird in the hand is worth two in the bush.

A closed mouth catches no flies.

A constant guest is never welcome.

A jack of all trades is master of none.

A penny saved is a penny earned.

A man is known by the company he keeps.

A picture is worth a thousand words.

A rolling stone gathers no moss.

A stitch in time saves nine.

A thief thinks everyone steals.

Actions speak louder than words.

All flowers are not in one garden.

All's fair in love and war.

All that glisters is not gold.

An early bird catches worms.

An Englishman's home is his castle.

An eye for an eye and a tooth for a tooth.

An eye for an eye leaves the whole world blind.

Ask me no questions, I'll tell you no lies.

As fit as a fiddle.

Homophones and neologisms

A homophone is a word that is pronounced the same as another word but differs in meaning.

Eye/ I

To / Two / Too

Brake / Break

Sauce/ Source

Aisle/ I'll/ Aisle

Cent /Scent/ Sent

Flour / Flower

Bury / Berry

Homophones of multiple words or phrases are also known as oronyms:

"ice cream" vs. "I scream"

"euthanasia" vs. "youth in Asia"

"some others" vs. "some mothers"

"night rain" vs. "night train"

A neologism is a newly coined word that may be in the process of entering common use, but has not yet been accepted into conventional language.

Laser

Staycation

Kleenex

Hoover

Meritocracy

Workaholic

Business English Writing

Masterclass International School

© Copyright 2020 - All rights reserved.

....

The content contained within this book may not be reproduced, duplicated or transmitted without direct written permission from the author or the publisher.

Under no circumstances will any blame or legal responsibility be held against the publisher, or author, for any damages, reparation, or monetary loss due to the information contained within this book. Either directly or indirectly.

Legal Notice:

This book is copyright protected. This book is only for personal use. You cannot amend, distribute, sell, use, quote or paraphrase any part, or the content within this book, without the consent of the author or publisher.

Disclaimer Notice:

Please note the information contained within this document is for educational and entertainment purposes only. All effort has been executed to present accurate, up to date, and reliable, complete information. No warranties of any kind are declared or implied. Readers acknowledge that the author is not engaging in the rendering of legal, financial, medical or professional advice. The content within this book has been derived from various sources. Please consult a licensed professional before attempting any techniques outlined in this book.

By reading this document, the reader agrees that under no circumstances is the author responsible for any losses, direct or indirect, which are incurred as a result of the use of information contained within this document, including, but not limited to, — errors, omissions, or inaccuracies.

Thank you for buying this book.

Made in the USA
Las Vegas, NV
13 October 2021